THE QUESTION MARK

HUGH MONTEFIORE

THE QUESTION MARK

The End of Homo Sapiens

The Theological Lectures 1969,
delivered under the auspices of the Church of Ireland
in Queen's University, Belfast

with a foreword by
DR JOSEPH NEEDHAM, FRS
Master of Gonville and Caius College,
Cambridge

COLLINS
ST JAMES'S PLACE, LONDON
1969

SBN 00 215671 7

© Hugh Montefiore, 1969

Printed in Great Britain by
Cox & Wyman Ltd,
London, Fakenham and Reading

FOR ELISABETH

CONTENTS

7

NOTE

These lectures were delivered at the Queen's University of Belfast in January 1969 under the general title 'Man's Dominion'. The papers are here published in their entirety and include some material not given in the original lectures owing to the exigencies of time as well as additional material made available since then.

PREFACE

I should like to record my gratitude to the many people who have assisted in the production of this book; first to my wife, who cheerfully suffered the loss of precious holiday time during the preparation of these lectures; to the Revd Cecil Kerr, Church of Ireland Dean of Residences at the Queen's University, Belfast, who invited me to give the Theological Lectures in 1969, and who made me so welcome during my visit; to the Vice-Chancellor of the Queen's University, the Archbishop of Armagh and Professor Charlton, who so kindly chaired the lectures; and to all those who have assisted me by their time and knowledge in fields where I am a complete amateur. In particular I should like to thank Dr Budowski of UNESCO, Dr Richard Holmes, Dr Henry Hulme, Professor Sir Joseph Hutchinson, Dr Malcolm Potts, Dr E. Schumacher, Dr Hans Selye, Mr J. Switzer, Professor W. H. Thorpe, Dr F. Arthur Vick and Mr Martin Wright. The responsibility for what I have written, however, must remain my own.

HUGH MONTEFIORE

'There is arising a crisis of world-wide proportions involving developing and developed countries alike – the crisis of the human environment. . . .
It is becoming apparent that, if current trends continue, the future of life on earth could be endangered.'

U THANT
Introduction to *Problems of the Human Environment*,
Report to the Forty-seventh Session of the United Nations,
26 May 1969

FOREWORD

It is an honour for me to have been asked by my old colleague as Dean of Caius, Hugh Montefiore, to write a few words in the front of his Belfast lectures. In Bernard Shaw's *Man and Superman* one of the characters sighs and remarks that 'things have never been the same since Professor Tyndall's lecture at Belfast' – perhaps the like will be said of these, or so I may be allowed to hope.

Theologians do not generally occupy themselves with the sort of questions to which Hugh Montefiore has applied his mind here, scientific, technological, medical and sociological questions affecting the entire future of mankind. The clergy seem to spend most of their time, at least in the eyes of the man in the street, continuing the scholastic debate about how many angels can dance on the point of a pin. Yet nothing could be more concerned with man in community, and man in relation to the Author of Nature, than a piercing look at the incredible wastage of natural resources, the heedless pollution of the environment, the dangers of unrestrained population pressure, the predictable neuroses of over-crowding on the earth's surface, the failure of food supplies to keep pace with humanity, and the ethical dangers of that biological engineering which the growth of natural know-ledge is daily bringing upon us.

Some people might wonder what religion in general and the Christian religion in particular has got to do with all this, but they would only be people who had never given any thought to what religion is really about. Montefiore has written some clarion phrases which will remain in the mind of the reader; he speaks of the necessity for a 'colossal effort of self-restraint' on the part of humanity, and a 'ceiling to the material standard of living' of the more highly privileged cultures. It is clearly necessary that the 'love of our neigh-bour' should be extended from our contemporaries in time to those many generations of men and women whom we ourselves shall never see. It is essential that Christians should finally free themselves from that preoccupation with indi-vidual salvation, that closed view of the universe, and that adherence to a body of doctrine impossible to believe today; otherwise they will never be able to leaven the world with the vision of the co-operative commonwealth of love, justice, comradeship and righteousness which mankind has in its power to bring about.

Of course I do not feel able to subscribe to all the points of view expressed by Hugh Montefiore. I am not quite happy about the emphasis on theism, for example, entirely valid though it is for those of us brought up within Christen-dom, Israel or Islam. In ancient China neither Confucianism nor Taoism was a theistic religion, yet some of the most interesting early examples of conscious nature-protection can be recorded from that civilization. Perhaps also we ought to study Asian attitudes to Nature much more closely, for oftentimes they were less aggressive regarding the 'lower creation' than those which derived from the Judaeo-Christian tradition. These may have had, as Lynn White thinks, some relation with the historical fact that *modern* science developed in Europe alone, but even if this were true it might well be that the dominating aggressiveness which was valuable four hundred years ago is now becoming a positive menace to the survival of all of us. Or again with regard to the doctrine of the Kingdom of God I feel more sympathy with Teilhard de Chardin's optimism than with Hugh Montefiore's pessimism; long ago I took my stand that we should think of it as 'here, but not yet', and work always for its coming.

These lectures raise political problems, though most of the time such issues have been left implicit. How far have the socialist countries been more conscientious about nature-conservation than the capitalist ones? The Kruschev dust-bowl was no doubt mainly a miscalculation, but the Lake Baikal fisheries seem not to have been saved in spite of vigorous protests by the scientists in Moscow. Yet would any socialist country engage in the stupendous waste repre-sented by the advertising 'industry' in the capitalist West, a waste responsible no doubt for the greater part of those 150 acres of forest mown down every week-end for a single Sunday newspaper? And there is wastage of a scandalous nature dictated by capitalist economics, not only the formerly much publicized burning of surplus coffee and foodstuffs, but more recently the destruction by the scrap-merchants of literally thousands of steam locomotives in perfect running condition, when all could have been usefully given away to the underpowered railway networks of the under-developed countries in Asia, Africa and Latin America. Christians cannot escape political duty, though all too often, alas, they fail to make their voices heard.

Yet my agreement with the Vicar of Great St Mary's is far broader than any reservations; and the main point is that so far as I can see as a scientist his analysis of the human predicament is entirely on the right lines. His three lectures seem to me brilliantly written and convincingly documented, and their influence will, I believe, be great. Nowadays a new Society for Social Responsibility in Science is being formed; may we not hope for some similar grouping of divines? At any rate I feel proud that a priest of the Church of England should thus lead the way in demonstrating so clearly one of the greatest tasks before contemporary society.

24 February 1969   JOSEPH NEEDHAM, FRS
                                     Master of Gonville and Caius College

Lecture One

THE FACTS OF THE CASE

It seems to me probable that the future of man as a species may be decided in the next half-century. This statement is made not as a prediction but as a prognosis. A prediction is a precise statement made on the basis of scientific experimentation which may be proved or disproved on scientific grounds. A prognosis is a personal judgement made about a man's future on the basis not only of past experience but the totality of evidence. No prediction about man's future is possible – there are too many unknown factors – and that is one of the reasons why most reputable scientists fight shy of this unpleasant subject. Cassandra would never have been a Fellow of the Royal Society. But this does not mean that there is no place for prognosis.[1] A sick man does not ignore his doctor because he gives a prognosis: and the same too should be true of a sick world.

The American cosmonauts, journeying to the moon and back, fired the imagination of the world. We live in a space age, with tangible proof of the wonders of science and technology. Those spacemen, looking at the small ball of earth spinning in space, were the first to see it 'as a single unified place of habitation'.[1A] We who live on 'the good earth' find it hard to look on our planet in this perspective: yet that is how it must be seen if we are to avoid the dangers which presently threaten it. The most important words of 1968 were not spoken by the American cosmonauts. They were in fact unreported by our press: they formed part of a speech made by Mr James Wiggins, US representative at the United Nations, at a plenary session on 3 December 1968:

I believe that the environmental problems . . . will appear, in the perspective of years, as of incomparably greater importance to the human species than the many political dissensions to which, because they arouse such dangerous passion, we must devote such a great part of our days and nights at the United Nations.

Why is this so important? Because the accredited spokesman of the most powerful nation on earth publicly admitted that, in the long term, the peacetime dangers to *Homo sapiens* are of 'incomparably greater importance' than the dangers of potential war. Now that is saying a very great deal. We are credibly informed that there is in the stockpiles of the nuclear powers at least 100 tons of TNT-equivalent in nuclear bombs for every man, woman and child on earth. According to a statement made by the Pentagon on 19 February 1968, the USA had at that time 4,200 multiple independent warheads for ICBMs, compared with Russia's 'somewhat less than 1,000'. The USA's superiority consisted in the greater armament of her submarine fleet. The ratio of superiority was expected to be maintained for the next six to eight years.[2] 'We could wipe out the human race and all our fellow lodgers the animals, the birds and the insects,

16

and reduce our planet to a radioactive desert.'[3] We are also informed that biological warfare experts can now prepare strains of virus bacteria to spread diseases against which defence preparations are almost impossible.[4] If the problems caused by peacetime living are as great as those caused by war, they must be very serious indeed.

It is my intention to devote these theological lectures to this problem. The first lecture will attempt as concise a statement of the problem as I can give. Since I am no scientist, and since it is not customary to take seriously the statements of theologians about science and technology, I shall attempt to quote authority for statements of fact. Subsequent lectures will be concerned with the nature of man, and his ability or inability to control his environment, and the third lecture will contain an examination of some theological aspects of man's problematical future.

The question mark over man's future has arisen because his increasing power over his environment has not been matched by increasing wisdom and restraint in its use. The needs of the moment have taken precedence over future consequences: the latter have been for the most part unknown and, if known, ignored. In particular physical changes have been effected without regard to their biological consequences.

All life on earth is confined to and dependent upon a thin film of air, soil and water known as the biosphere. As human evolution has developed, man's role in the biosphere has changed:

With the discovery of the uses of fire he was able to modify vegetation and thus affect the conditions of life for a much wider array of plants and animals. With the development of domestication he emerged from being simply another kind of omnivorous animal to become a factor determining the conditions of life for all other species inhabiting the same geographical area. With civilization and the gradual development of technological skills he became a minor geological force, affecting that portion of biosphere in which his numbers were concentrated. With the industrial revolution and the channelling of new energy sources into the production of materials useful to himself, he became a global force, and assumed a position of ecological dominance over other living components and much of the inorganic material of the biosphere.

Despite this however man remains basically an omnivorous animal dependent upon the oxygen and water from the atmosphere, and energy from sunlight transformed by green plants into states suitable for human capture and assimilation. Although in a position of dominance, he cannot for long modify conditions within the biosphere beyond the limits of tolerance for himself and the animals and plants upon which he still depends for life. Where he does so, he perishes.[5]

As the Final Report of the UNESCO conference held in Paris in September 1968[6] makes clear, there is

a new awareness of the loss of environmental quality . . . throughout the world. Although some of the changes in the environment have been taking place for decades or longer, they seem to have reached a threshold of criticalness.[7]

The problems may be considered under three broad heads; resources, pollution and health. The complexity of the subject is caused by the interdependence of man with all his environment, and the interconnectedness of many different and apparently separate subjects.

The technological revolution has enabled man to exploit the resources of the world as never before; and this has been done on the basis of profitability without regard for posterity. There have been great gains in comfort and convenience, health and happiness. There has also been terrifying waste. For example, Mr Wiggins, of the USA, speaking of his country alone, has said:

Every year this nation discards 7 million automobiles, 20 million tons of paper, 48,000 million cans, 26,000 million bottles and jars. Much of this material, made of aluminium and plastics, is virtually proof against decay. One wonders what archaeologists of some future age will think of us when they dig these things up.[8]

If natural resources were limitless, this would only have nuisance value. Unfortunately, they are not limitless.

In a lecture such as this, it is only possible to mention a few of these valuable resources. I instance here only water, soil, animals, trees and fossil fuel.

The world is running short of fresh water. It has been reckoned that there are 326 million cubic miles of water in this planet, of which 97.2 per cent is in the oceans, and 2.15 per cent in glaciers and ice-caps.[9] Only when cheap nuclear power makes desalination economically feasible on a gigantic scale (and as yet there is no hint of this) will the world's water supplies be assured. (At a public inquiry held at Llandovery in 1966–7, it was reckoned that the cost of desalinated water from a nuclear-powered unit would be nearly three times that of water from a regulating reservoir.

According to Professor R. S. Silver, the cost was unlikely to fall below 4s. 6d. per thousand gallons. A report on desalination from our Water Resources Board is expected in the summer of 1969.) 'The condition of mankind after only two or three decades of the present population increase will depend heavily with respect to water resources on the success of national and international programmes of research development, staff training and public education.'[10] The problem of water shortage is partly one of pollution, and partly one of population, but the lion's share of water requirements is for industry, as the following figures show. To make 1 ton of human tissue, 10 tons of water is required. But the equivalent of paper requires 250 tons, of fertilizer 600 tons, and of refined sugar 1,000 tons.[11] Industrial re-use of water would no doubt mitigate (but not solve) the problem. Already some areas of the world are living heavily on a water deficit. For example, in Los Angeles and neighbouring California, a thousand times more water is being consumed than is being precipitated.[12] The World Hydrological Decade started in 1965. It has not made much progress to date.

The destruction of precious soil is no speciality of the present century. The Fertile Crescent is now a sandy waste. The granary of Rome is now the desert of North Africa. The American dust-bowl was the product of the nineteenth century. But, with a rising population, the world can no longer afford soil erosion. We cannot afford to reach the point of no return, when a tough layer of laterite occurs and soil recovery is no longer possible.[13] This is the danger threatening the recently destroyed forests of the Amazon. Mr Kruschev's policy of ploughing up the virgin lands of Kazahkstan without adequate protection against soil erosion has turned 50 million acres into dust-bowls, according to the Russian journal *Moskva*.[14] Much soil has also been lost through ill-advised methods of cultivation and irrigation, which bring to the surface salts which deaden the soil. Mankind is faced by the fact of a daily deficit of 830,000 acres.[15] It takes hundreds of years for nature to produce one inch of humus with its highly complex components.[16]

A particularly serious result of the growing needs of man has been the destruction of forests. Trees are important because their root system holds the soil and traps water. Rainfall, trapped in the trees, evaporates, and so produces further precipitation.[17] The leaves manure the ground.[18] Where the ground water has sunk below a certain level, there is no chance of planting a forest. In 1963 it was reported that the annual deficit of timber was a billion cubic metres.[19] A single Sunday edition of the *New York Times* eats up 150 acres of forest land.[20] In 1950 it was estimated that 40 per cent of the tropical forest zone had been cleared in Africa, and that by 1955 40 per cent of Brazil's forests had been cleared within the last quarter-century.[21]

One of the effects of intensive cultivation to feed the growing population of the world is the destruction of wild-life. Animals tend to become extinct when deprived of either their habitat or their food, or when they are killed in large numbers (usually for food, sometimes for sport).[22] At an earlier stage in man's development, he appears to have ruthlessly exterminated species. 'Recent work on the so-called "Pleistocene overkill" goes so far as to suggest that man exterminated nearly half the larger mammals in Africa some 50,000 years ago, and that in North Africa (where man arrived much later) he similarly killed off at least sixty per cent of the species of large mammals around 10,000 B.C.'[23] During the last 2,000 years alone some one hundred different forms of mammal have become extinct in various parts of the world; but by now the rate has been speeded up to something like one mammal a year![24] What is more, in June 1967, 271 mammals were officially listed as in danger of extinction.[25] In the six months since then, the number has increased to 275.[26] These are only the species threatened with extinction: many more have been gravely reduced. Quite apart from the moral and aesthetic problems of man's right to destroy species, extinction is serious for a number of reasons. Wildlife is part of the ecosystems on which man depends. A variety of forms improves the chance of survival if there is need of adaptation to new conditions.[27] 'Diversity of environments is of crucial importance for the evolution of man and his societies because the ultimate result of a stereotyped and equalized environment can be and often is an impoverishment of life.'[28] The protein potential of wildlife is valuable in areas where cultivation would not be economic.[29]

Perhaps the most valuable of all the earth's resources to have been exhausted in a comparatively fleeting moment will be the fossil fuels: coal, oil, petrol and natural gas. Accumulated over millions of years, they will have been

mostly used up within a couple of centuries. They contain
the earth's treasury of heat/energy, derived, as all our energy
must be, from the sun. By photosynthesis the forests of
earth and sea amassed their store of carbons and, buried deep
under pressure in the earth, they have kept this heritage
intact until man came to exploit it. It is not known what are
the real future resources of these energy-producing fuels.
The known proven resources, at the present rate of use, are
estimated as follows: coal 2,000 years, natural gas up to
30 years, oil (in December 1967) 31·7 years.[30] If the present
plan to manufacture synthetic protein from fossil fuels is
commercially successful, no doubt these fuels will disappear
more quickly. (Their products are also used for the manufacture of plastics.) At present there is overproduction of most
of these fuels, and no impediment, other than that of price, is
placed on their exploitation. The present publicity accorded
to North Sea gas has blinded most people to the simple
truth that, on present discoveries, there is enough gas to
supply Britain for less than a generation, or for less if the
exhortations of *The Times* be heeded. 'To get the best out of
North Sea gas for the nation it must be used in quantity.
Britain must burn several times as much gas as at present.'[31]
When these fossil fuels are exhausted, there will be com-
parable sources of nuclear fuel. Although the new gas
centrifuge has eased the problem of concentrating uranium
235, some doubt has been expressed about the availability of
sufficient stocks of this fissile material. The introduction of
advanced gas-cooled reactors means that by 1971 nuclear
power stations will be producing power at a marginally

cheaper rate than those which produce conventional fuels,[32] but the proven resources of uranium are insufficient to supply their needs beyond 1980.[33] There are said to be 4,000 million tons of uranium dissolved in the sea,[34] but, although Harwell scientists have recovered one gram of uranium from sea water, extraction is as yet quite uneconomic from a commercial point of view.[35]

Uranium will be much more efficiently and economically used when fast breeder reactors, of which a prototype is now under construction in Scotland, begin to generate power (although this will not be before 1980). These reactors can utilize the uranium taken out of fuel elements when they have completed their useful life in Magnox and advanced gas-cooled reactors. A fast breeder reactor can actually produce more plutonium than it consumes, with the result that the generating cost of producing electricity will be cut and the useful life of existing uranium stocks can be extended: and so when they come into production, crises may well be averted. (In any case uranium and its products are not the only available sources of fuel for nuclear fission. Other fuel cycles are being explored, using for example thorium, of which there are large deposits; and the possibility of power from the nuclear fusion of light elements cannot be ruled out.)

All this however lies in the future. At present there is no breakthrough to unlimited cheap nuclear power: that must wait upon the more successful application of fusion techniques to peacetime needs. Today in Britain 'there are large numbers of coal-fired units under construction that will be burning coal at the end of the century. . . . The fuel supply situation cannot be changed overnight'.[36] In 1966 the world had only eighty-three atomic generating plants in operation, and it was calculated that the amount of nuclear power would double every three and a half years.[37] Perhaps the transition from conventional to nuclear power can be made smoothly, but posterity is bound to question man's blind rape of the irreplaceable fossil fuels.

Mankind is not merely using up valuable raw materials without thought for posterity: he is also polluting his environment with their by-products. This pollution can affect the natural growth of vegetation, the well-being of the animal world and the health of our whole species. Pollution is found in the earth and the air and the water – and also now in space. It is caused by pesticides, by industrial processes and the internal-combustion engine, and by nuclear experiment and nuclear waste. How serious is this pollution? The Final Report of the Biosphere Conference has the following:

Delegates confirmed that pollution is one of the major problems facing humanity at present and that it may ultimately be important in limiting the earth's population through deterioration of man's physical and mental health.[38]

The situation is serious, but not irremediable if a great effort is made.

If mankind is prepared to make a determined effort, to support much more research to make that effort effective, our descendants may not be condemned to live on an impoverished planet devoid of so much of the varied life which has made it so interesting and so beautiful.[39]

Mankind has always been plagued with pests, and, ever since the introduction of fire, human beings have begun to dominate their environment, and so to eradicate them. Settled agriculture meant the encouragement of certain plants, and the discouragement of pests and weeds. The development of technology and the growth of industrial manufacture by mass-production methods has meant a colossal increase in industrial wastes, while the mass production of motor-cars adds further pollution to the atmosphere. 'In the United States a baby is born every twelve seconds and a car every five seconds.'[40] 'Increase in solid wastes in USA and Europe are reckoned at about 2 % p.a.'[41] Pests are still a serious cause of loss to agriculture (£300 million is lost to British agriculture alone each year on this account);[42] and so stronger and stronger pesticides have been produced.

The problems of nuclear waste, although they do not at the moment cause anxiety, pose very serious dangers for the future, especially as the demand for power is increasing on an exponential curve, and (unless this earth is to return to a primitive level of power) nuclear power will have to take over increasingly from the fossil fuels as they become exhausted. Pollution by fall-out, although it could devastate the world in the grip of a nuclear war, has not seriously affected the environment to date, since it is equivalent to only about one eightieth of the natural radiation background.[43] (The amount of deaths from leukaemia and other forms of cancer that this additional radiation has caused is unknown.) Pollution through accidents should not be forgotten. The Spanish Supreme Court dismissed the appeal of the Duchess of Medina Sidonia against a sentence of one year's imprisonment for leading a march protesting that the USA had paid inadequate compensation for damage caused by the hydrogen bomb that fell in the area of Palomares from a crashing US bomber during 1967.[44] It is reported that the area of North Star Bay, Greenland, where a jet carrying four hydrogen bombs crashed on 22 January 1968 is now safe. 'All sensitive material has been picked up. Only fragments of the H. Bombs were recovered. The rest of the debris is, presumably, still in the area.'[45] Lord Ritchie-Calder describes the result of the Windscale accident in 1957. 'Milk was dumped into the sea because radioactive iodine had got into the dairy pastures.'[46] On 14 February 1968 Sweden complained to the USA and Russia that radioactivity was leaking into the atmosphere from underground tests in addition to fall-out. The extent of this is either unknown or kept secret.

As for the radioactive effluent of nuclear generating stations, 'at the present writing, no procedures for ultimate disposal of such high-level wastes is as yet available'.[47] Incorporation into glass has been proposed.[48] Disposal at sea may be the answer to certain low-activity waste[49] but difficulties of surveillance and dumping are obvious. Lord Ritchie-Calder has described the American method of 'disposal by injection' of high-activity waste which otherwise would remain radioactive more than 250,000 years, longer than the containers in which it is placed.[50] However, this method 'would only be applied in very special cases where all the necessary geological conditions obtained locally'.[51] The matter is becoming urgent. 'The rapid, ex-

tensive development of nuclear power will very soon result
in a growing output of waste whose specific radioactivity will
bear no relation to that of today's waste.'[52] In this situation
one serious suggestion has been made that the waste should
be stored in liquid form for a period of several decades,
'deferring any better solution to a better day'.[53] Charming
for posterity!

Radioactivity is only one form of pollution. Water
pollution has been with us for centuries but, with increasing
population, the problem has increased. Exclusive of industrial
wastes, the amount of organic and mineral pollutants in
water has been estimated at 10 litres of wet sludge per capita
daily, or 50 kilograms per capita of dry solids annually.[54] In
some areas the process of pollution has been accelerated by
'eutrophication'. 'Certain wastes from homes and industries
– for instance, synthetic detergents – may fertilize lakes and
rivers to such an extent that, ironically, they ultimately die.'[55]
Other pollutants cause the death of the food off which fish
feed, and thus the death of the fish themselves. The most
famous example is Lake Erie in America. In 1956 the blue
pike catch alone amounted to just short of 7 million pounds.
Today if you fall from a boat into the lake, you are advised
to have a tetanus injection.[56] A study of the situation carried
out by the *Wall Street Journal* quotes the opinion of scientists
to the effect that the lake may be 'on the verge of a biological
cataclysm'.[57] The problem is not confined to America. In
Western Europe the Rhine is badly polluted, and in Russia
even Lake Baikal has begun to be affected.[58] Filtering is only
effective against certain pollutants.[59] On 8 January 1969

Dr K. Mellanby was reported in *The Times* to have said that nitrate had been detected in water up to 30 parts per million. a level poisonous for babies up to nine months old.

The general public was first alerted to the dangers of pesticides, especially chlorinated hydrocarbons, by Rachel Carson's *Silent Spring*.[60] This book confined itself to the American scene: but the problem is becoming world-wide.

Great anxiety was expressed in respect to indiscriminate use of pesticides, especially the chlorinated insecticides which persist in living organisms and often prove to be deleterious to animals and man at the top of certain food chains.[61]

Some of these chlorinated compounds appear resistant to biological destruction.[62]

DDT has been found even in penguins in the Antarctic.[63] A sample of Scottish porpoises showed concentrations of 25 parts per million of DDT in fatty tissues, more than six times the concentration found in man.[64] The discrepancy is explained by the different length of their respective food chains. The leaching of soil leading to water pollution is inevitable, and marine life throughout the world is bound to be polluted. The Baltic has been polluted by DDT to such a level that it is dangerous to eat certain fish regularly, according to a research team acting for the Swedish Institute of Public Health.[65] Vital organs may be affected at times of stress when fat is concerted into food.[66] More serious, perhaps, is the possible effect of DDT on algae. 'According to a scientific report issued in the spring of 1968, 1/1000 of a gram of DDT in 1,000 kilograms of water may lower the metabolism of the algae by 75 per cent. This would be a direct threat to the life of the algae, since hundreds of thousands of tons of DDT are spread over the continents every year, of which a major part ultimately finds its way to the oceans. Global oxygen production depends largely on photosynthesis of oceanic plancton and algae. We may thus endanger even the critically important oxygen content of the air.[67] 'It is generally agreed among scientists who have considered the origin of life on earth that before life evolved, the earth's atmosphere was devoid of oxygen.'[68] Oxygen is produced by organisms, and algae are so important for its production because of the preponderance of sea over land on our planet. Since all marine organisms depend on algae, their life too may be endangered.[69] So all life on earth is imperilled by DDT! At present the use of DDT is unrestricted in Britain. DDT is now banned in Sweden and Michigan (USA). Its use in England is presently under review.

Pollution of the atmosphere has been with us since the industrial revolution. But it is getting worse, and unless drastic steps are taken it will become still worse, since it is reckoned that in the industrial countries 'the next 20 years will see probably a doubling of industrial production with corresponding potential air pollutant emissions, unless substantial countermeasures are taken'.[70]

Although pollution of the atmosphere would seem to be a local matter, in fact toxic materials can be carried long distances in the atmosphere. Sweden has complained about the dangerously high level of methylated mercury in fish caught in certain lakes, brought by air from outside its frontiers.[71] Pollutants come from Germany, possibly from Great Britain as well.[72] Plant life is affected chiefly by sulphur dioxide in relatively low concentrations.[73] As for human beings, it has long been known that air pollutants cause chronic bronchitis.[74] There is a correlation between the emission of lead through exhaust gases (1 kilogram per vehicle per annum) and the content of lead in man, which may, if steps are not taken, reach a toxic level.[75] Carbon monoxide from exhaust gases 'may well prove to be a critical substance in city air'.[76] The London smog of 1952, as a result of which some 4,000 people died, had a high content of soot[77] while Los Angeles smog is caused by chemical action on exhaust gases.[78] A causal connection between air pollutants and lung cancer is suspected by many experts.[79]

The immensity of the problem is seen by the fact that every year, in the United States alone, '142 million tons of smoke and noxious fumes – over 1,400 pounds *per capita* – are dumped annually into the atmosphere'.[80]

One particular pollutant, if it be right to call it that, must be noted, because its possible effects are as portentous as those of DDT. The rapid combustion of fossil fuels in the last century has meant that the carbon dioxide content of the atmosphere has increased by 10 per cent.[81] ('A four-engined jet passenger aircraft in normal flight emits about two and two thirds tons of carbon dioxide and one and one third ton of water vapour every ten minutes!'[82]) The content is increasing at the rate of ·7 parts per million each year.[83] When all the known reserves of fossil fuel have been burnt, the concentration will be ten times greater.[84] This suggests that 'the buffering action' of the oceans (which can store carbon dioxide) has not been able to keep pace with the increase.[85] From this Lord Ritchie-Calder has drawn certain conclusions.[86] If consumption of fossil fuels continues at the present rate of increase, the mean annual temperature of the world might increase by 3·6 degrees centigrade in the next forty to fifty years. The north polar ice-cap is shrinking and thinning. Marine plant life is increasing, and thus adding further to the carbon dioxide released in the atmosphere. As a result fish are migrating. (On 3 January 1969 it was stated by the European Inland Fisheries Commission of FAO that thermal discharges into rivers from industrial and nuclear plants are threatening freshwater fish; so rivers are at danger too.) In Scandinavia land is thawing and arrowheads over 1,000 years old are being exposed. Lord Ritchie-Calder believes that flooding may become catastrophic and that patterns of rainfall may change. Not all would accept this prophecy – some believe that increased carbon dioxide in the atmosphere may tend to blanket the sun's rays – but it is not a consideration that can be ignored.

Finally one last area of pollution must be mentioned – space. In a lecture in Manchester on 19 February 1968 Sir Bernard Lovell drew attention to the dangers of space pollution. He was principally concerned with the dangers of misidentification of space debris for nuclear missiles, but he drew attention to the potential danger of space probes bringing contamination by microbes to outer space; and he pointed out that there were then 1,291 large objects known to him to be orbiting the earth and liable to return to its surface.[87] He said that the consumption of fuel by space rockets reduced the ozone layer, and that this might possibly affect the amount of cosmic rays which reach the earth. The ionosphere could be disrupted. Lord Ritchie-Calder has drawn attention[88] to the hydrogen bomb which was detonated in the Van Allen belt of the earth's atmosphere during the International Geophysical Year 1957/8. 'We still do not know,' he wrote, 'the cost we may have to pay for this artificial magnetic disturbance.'[88A]

All these pollutants are potentially dangerous. Some will definitely be dangerous unless energetic countermeasures are taken soon. They are all examples of the way in which man affects his environment without taking thought for the biological effects he may be causing.

The dangers to man lie in the results these pollutants may have on health. But there are other factors affecting health, the most important of which is malnutrition or even starvation resulting from insufficient food of the right kind for an exploding world population. According to the figures released by the Population Reference Bureau in Washington on 10 March 1968, the world's population on 1 January 1968 was estimated at 3,443 million. By this year the 3,500 million mark is expected to have been reached, and the world population is expected to reach 4,500 million by 1983, and 7,000 million by the millennium. (It is interesting to note that previous estimates made from the UN Demographic Yearbook have had to be revised not downwards but upwards.) The increase is spotlighted by the fact that, according to the calculations of the Population Reference Bureau, during 1968 there were 225 births per minute, but only 93 deaths. The imbalance is caused not by an increase in birth-rate but because in developing countries the birth-rate has not followed down the death-rate, as it has in the developed countries. Thus, while the world's annual rate of population increase for this decade is 1·9 per cent, in Europe it is only ·9 per cent while in Latin America it is 2·8 per cent. (Infant mortality in the more developed countries is about 20 per 1,000 or less, whereas in the developing countries it fluctuates between 200 and 300 per 1,000. Expectation of life in the former is around 70, compared with 45 in the developing countries.[89]) As a result of the population increase, one third of the world's population is said to be under sixteen. The exponential curve of the world's exploding population can be seen in the fact that it took until the early nineteenth century to reach the first billion of the world's population, another century to add the second billion, but now it takes only fifteen years to add a further billion to our world population.

Is it possible to feed these vast numbers? The problem is only partly regional, pinpointed by the Common Market proposal to feed back surplus butter to cows, which strikes a rather lunatic note.[90] In the developed countries ironically enough overeating is becoming the problem. 'The high level of prosperity is creating a new set of medical problems.'[91] It is estimated that in the last two decades their peoples have added 300 calories per day to their diets without taking correspondingly greater exercise.[92] In the developing countries, however, there is chronic undernourishment, and when there is a bad harvest, as in 1965, actual famine. Whereas the developed countries have increased their yields of crops, in India the wheat yield is the same as it was sixty years ago, and the rice yield is actually down,[93] although the areas under cultivation have risen. Fortunately experiments have recently produced high-yielding wheat in Mexico and rice in the Philippines, and this gives some ground for hope. (The suggestion that the hungry millions may be fed with protein extracted from leaves is more ingenious than practical.[94])

It is generally assumed that there is a drastic protein shortage in the developing countries. The Director-General of the FAO however denies this,[95] and insists that the protein shortage among the poor is due to the fact that the rich eat more than their fair share of this necessary dietary component. Similarly he is optimistic about averting future world famine. 'I would like to state firmly that the FAO has no statistical evidence suggesting that the world is proving incapable of feeding a rising population.'[96] (Other authorities however are less sanguine.[97]) Mr Boerma does however admit that there is no clear answer to the demand for improving the present inadequate subsistence level diet of the undernourished millions. Others who have studied the relation of fertilizers to agriculture are certain that it will prove impossible to meet an increase of food production over an extended period at the rate of 3 to 4 per cent.[98]

If the rising population of the world raises a question

mark over the world's food resources, it also affects the conditions under which men live. Whereas in 1920 only some 360 million were living in cities, it is estimated that by the year 2000 the number will have increased eightfold to 3,000 million.[99] Put it this way. In the developed regions, whereas in 1920 two out of every five were living in towns, this number will have increased by the year 2000 to four out of every five.[100] 'Man is a gregarious animal: he generally tends to accept crowded environments and even to seek them.'[101] Lord Ritchie-Calder calls this 'Hell upon Earth'. It seems inevitable.

Life in cities involves increased pressure and stress, and can cause anxiety, so that in three years there have been 43 million prescriptions on the NHS alone for psychotropic drugs.[102] On the other hand, as Professor López Ibor commented at a World Psychiatric Association symposium, 'Man needs normal anxiety'.[103] Furthermore, a high correlation has been noted between national levels of anxiety and economic growth rates![104] It has even been suggested that lung cancer is less likely among the neurotic.[105]

But there is another side to the picture. One of the drawbacks of technology and mass production is that they may remove from man the stimulus and variety necessary to realize his full potential. 'While protection from stress and from effort may add to the pleasure or at least to the comfort of the moment, and while emotional neutrality minimises social conflicts, the consequences of an excessively sheltered life are almost certainly unfavourable in the long run. They are even dangerous in that man becomes adjusted to a particular place and time but loses his ability to readjust as surroundings change.'[106] 'It is high time that we made a deliberate effort to create and maintain as diversified an environment as possible, even though this results in some loss in efficiency, in order to provide the soil for the many kind of seeds now dormant in man's nature.'[107] Experiments on rats have shown that under conditions of overcrowding leading to social stress, death has occurred without wounding.[108] However, the suicide rates of the world, contrary to popular belief, have remained pretty steady over the last sixty years. Switzerland was top of the league in 1901 with 22·4 per 100,000, and had dropped back by 1964 to 17. In England the rate, which was 9·6 in 1901, rose to 11·7 in 1964. (These figures come from the WHO and British official sources.) Even student suicide rates in the post-war period, while they have increased in Cambridge, show a 50 per cent decrease at Oxford.[109] Furthermore, according to the 1961 census, the Greater London area had a lighter mortality rate than that of England and Wales as a whole. So much for London overcrowding! But there may be special factors here,[110] since this was not true of England's other conurbations, all of which had a death-rate above the national average.[111]

Dr Selye, who has made a lifelong study of stress, defines it as 'the rate of wear and tear in the body'.[112] He has even been able to measure stress clinically by what he has called the 'general adaptation syndrome',[113] and he has isolated particular stress illnesses as well as relating stress to all disease.[114] Although stress illnesses (for example heart disease, hypertension, rheumatoid infections and stomach ulcers) are much in the news, it must be remembered that this is due in part, perhaps totally, to the fact that specific disease-killers have declined at a phenomenal rate. There is however need for vigilance. There has been a recrudescence of malaria in Ceylon and cholera in a new form is knocking at the portals of Europe.[115] The use of antibiotics in factory farming may produce new viruses which antibiotics cannot overcome.[116] Certainly increased stress has not reduced the expectation of life in the USA: on the contrary, it has grown from 48 years in 1900 to 69·8 in 1956.[117] But expectation of life is not to be equated with health and happiness.

If however stress has not reduced life-span, it can have other undesirable effects. Professor Wynne-Edwards has recently put forward the hypothesis, and corroborated it with an overwhelming mass of facts, that density regulation, and through this control of numbers, is the main function of social organization in animals.[118] Considerable evidence has been adduced to indicate that animals show symptoms of increased stress under overcrowded conditions, and also that fighting often occurs under these conditions. The intensity of conflict increases with population density.[119] In 1957 P. Leyhausen had suggested, as a result of his study of captive cat and wolf communities, that space in its physical or so to say biological form (and not merely in a sublimated or figurative sense) is indispensable for the biological and particularly for the psychological and mental health of humans in a human society.[120] From his observation of solitary mammals he further suggested that human beings have inherited in their nature a combination of both a territorial dominance and also a relative hierarchical dominance, so that either a *laisser-faire* society or a dictatorship, such as appear inevitable in overcrowded conditions, is alien to human nature and produces stress symptoms of aggression.[121] Thus overcrowding might well account for increased delinquency. According to figures extracted from the relevant volumes of *Criminal Statistics, England and Wales* and the Census Reports of the Registrar-General, indictable crimes recorded by the police increased from 80,962 in 1901 (with a population of $32\frac{1}{2}$ million) to 1,133,382 in 1965 (with a population of nearly 48 million.[122]) McClintock and Avison note that trends in urbanisation and in increase of recorded crime are in the same direction.[123] Overcrowding might well account for other contemporary phenomena of urban societies, such as sexual promiscuity, withdrawal from society (typified by 'hippies' on the one hand and anarchists and student revolutionaries on the other) and political apathy.[124] W. M. S. and C. Russell claim that almost every major war in world history can be traced back to a population crisis.[125] Professor Calhoun and others have shown that crowded conditions can seriously disturb maternal care in rats and mice[126] and if this occurs among humans, the resulting psychological scars can affect later behaviour. 'Granted that the pathological consequences of crowding are not yet understood ... in most cases the effects of crowding will be found to have an insidious course ... (mostly) by the secondary responses evoked from the whole organism and from the whole social group.'[127]

Such are the warning lights over man's future which we have briefly examined under the heading of resources, pollution and health. On the one hand man has always lived under 'unnatural conditions'. 'Ever since the late Palaeolithic and especially Neolithic times he has been living physically, mentally and socially a kind of existence that has changed and still is changing too fast to permit his adjustment through biological evolution.'[128] On the other hand, 'it is an illusion that man could enlarge the range of his genetic adaptabilities and thus escape from the bondage of his evolutionary past. Man can function only to the extent that he maintains or creates around himself a micro-environment within the range of his natural tolerance'.[129]

I make no apology for using this first lecture for setting before you a sombre and perhaps startling outline of the facts of mankind's present dilemma. It is too often thought that ethics and theology are abstract disciplines divorced from the facts of life. On the contrary, ethics and theology concern the life of the world. On the basis of these facts, I shall go on to ask in the next two lectures whether man in his present predicament has further need of God. If this be the world that I have described, in what sense can we say Christ is the hope of the world, and in what sense can we assert that Christ is the way, the truth and the life? How can the Christian faith help us to overcome our dangers? To these questions I turn in succeeding lectures.

Lecture delivered 27 January 1969, under the title 'Human Nature and the Future'.

Lecture Two

THE ONLY HOPE

In the first of these lectures, I drew attention to the question mark which hangs over the future of *Homo sapiens* by reason of man's exploding population and his manipulation of his environment. I would like to start this lecture by quoting some words of Arthur Koestler:[1]

There are two reasons which entitle us to call our time 'unique'. The first is quantitative, expressed by the exponential increase of populations, communications, destructive power, etc. Under their combined impact, an extra-terrestrial intelligence, to whom centuries are as seconds, able to survey the whole curve in one sweep, would probably come to the conclusion that human civilisation is either on the verge of, or in the process of, exploding.

The second reason is qualitative, and can be summed up in a single sentence: before the thermonuclear bomb, man had to live with the idea of his death as an individual; from now onward, mankind has to live with the idea of its death as a species.

While Koestler's statement is undoubtedly correct, he seems to me to have underestimated (or perhaps not realized) that man's peacetime activities are in the long run as dangerous as, or perhaps even more dangerous than possible future warfare.

What is to be done in this situation? The first necessity would seem to be to state the problem. Until that is done there is no hope whatsoever that it may be resolved. Who will do this? Unfortunately human ecology as a discipline does not seem to attract many brilliant young men. Nobody admires a Cassandra. A young scientist, choosing his department of research, is more likely to opt for a field where he can make his name by creative brilliance. Ecology is a synthesizing discipline. 'The problems which mankind faces in this area cannot be tackled piecemeal. The biosphere, and man's place in it, must be envisaged as a whole.'[2] Ecology differs from the natural sciences in as much as it cannot offer prediction but only prognosis. The complexity of the issues does not permit precise results. This does not detract from its validity or from its utility, but it frightens away people who know that in the past many false prognoses have been made.

It is most unfortunate that the kind of facts which I gathered for the first lecture are not easily accessible.[3] It is extraordinary that an overworked parish priest who is an amateur on the subject should have to attempt to assemble them. One would have thought that scientists themselves would have collected them. I fear that many scientists do not really want the average citizen to appraise their work. Yet the adverse results of science and technology affect the citizen as much as the scientist. Here I would like to quote the words of Professor Barry Commoner:[4]

The scientist does have an urgent duty to *help* society solve the grave problems that have been created by the progress of science.

But the problems are social and must be solved by social processes. In these processes the scientist has one vote and no claim to leadership beyond that given to *any* person who has the gift of moving his fellow men. But the citizen, and the government official, whose task it is to make the judgements, cannot do so in the absence of the necessary facts and relevant evaluations. Where these are matters of science, the scientist as the custodian of this knowledge has a profound duty to impart as much of it as he can to his fellow citizens. But in doing so, he must guard against false pretensions and avoid claiming for science that which belongs to the conscience. By this means scientists can place the decisions on the grave issues which they have helped to create in the proper hands – the hands of an informed citizenry.

A great debt is owed to UNESCO for summoning the Biosphere Conference in Paris during September 1968, and thereby pinpointing attention on these issues, and helping to make available facts about our rapidly changing environment. No doubt, when the United Nations takes up the matter at the 1972 Conference which – momentously – they have agreed to hold on this urgent subject, more publicity will be given to some of the disturbing facts of man's irresponsibility to which I drew attention in my first lecture. That will be all to the good. It will help to dispel the kind of complacency that led Robert Arvill to write in his best-selling book: 'the activities of leaders in all sectors of society give hope that man is responding to the challenge of his powers'.[5]

I would not wish, however, to appear to apportion blame exclusively to scientists. I fear that my own profession has been equally slow to grasp the importance of these issues.

Religious leaders in the West, despite biblical warnings, have been inclined to swim with the tide of increasing material affluence. The minds of theologians are far too much turned inwards to problems of Christology and to matters concerning the Church and the sacraments. Of course it would be wrong to suggest that such matters are unimportant. But it is small wonder that theology is regarded by so many as irrelevant if it does not concern itself with the moral and theological implications of what is happening in the real world in which we all live. I am particularly grateful for the opportunity to deliver these Theological Lectures here in Belfast, and for the suggestion that I should speak about this subject, because of the stimulus it has afforded to do further work upon the problem.[6]

I hope that I will not seem ungrateful to UNESCO if my next words appear critical. Again and again their publications speak of a 'rational use of resources'. For example, the Final Report of the Biosphere Conference has this sentence:

A rationalization of use of the resources of the biosphere on a world-wide scale is imperative if satisfactory living conditions of future generations are to be guaranteed.[7]

As a statement this is admirable; but it leaves the impression that if only a rational solution is found, men will take it. Alas, this is not the case. Man so often acts irrationally. Fortunately there is a hint that the conference realised that more than rationality is involved. It was agreed in the Final Report that

44

Natural science and technology alone are inadequate for modern solutions to resource management problems.[8]

The authors of some of the papers for the conference occasionally went even further. Thus, Mr Guy Gresford wrote:

In recent times, man has tended to become so dominant on Earth that he is now approaching a position where he constitutes one of the principal aspects of his own environment and in which environmental mastery would require the subjugation even of human nature by man. The resolution of this situation is a philosophical problem, which requires a restatement of the humanist objectives in new terms on which we can agree or acquiesce.[9]

The author of this paper is wrong. The resolution of this situation is not a philosophical problem. Philosophy, in the traditional use of the word, provides only a way of looking at life. But the dangers imperilling the world require more than a *Weltanschauung*. They need action, and the motive power of such action is not philosophical but religious, whether it be a humanist and non-theistic religion (such as is loosely called humanism), or whether it be a theistic and supernatural religion such as Christianity.

The first question of all to be asked is whether or not we have any duty towards posterity. I do not myself think that any answer can be given to this question from mere humanism. René Dubos has written:[10]

There is a good deal of evidence to suggest that a society which loses its identity with posterity and which loses its positive image of the future also loses its capacity to deal with present problems and soon falls apart.

This provides a quite inadequate reason for mankind's concern for posterity. The possible effect on present problems of man's lack of concern for the future could never sufficiently be a motive power which would arouse the world to take exceptional and unprecedented action. I understand that a humanist philosopher might find two ways in which to justify mankind's duty towards posterity; one, that it is the nature of the case (i.e. people do in fact have this feeling of obligation), and the other, because such an attitude of mind towards the welfare of posterity is a 'blik' capable of universalisation. However, the fact that an attitude is capable of being universalised does not necessarily imply that it *ought* to be universalised. Furthermore it is not immediately apparent that all people do have a feeling of obligation for the welfare of posterity. No doubt we are a mixture of good and bad, and in any case it is natural for a man to look a couple of generations or so ahead, so that his children and grand-children may be reasonably safe; but, beyond that, man is likely to comfort himself with the thought that something will turn up (it always has before), and that future generations must take their chance.

Humanists have a real concern for human values and respect human personality. Naturally they have a humane attitude towards future generations. For them it would be a tragedy if the future should be so heavily mortgaged. It would be a tragedy if human values were seriously threatened. But tragedy and compassion are not the same as moral obligation and response. It is not clear why humanists, on their own assumptions, should believe that mankind *as a whole* has a moral obligation towards posterity, nor is it clear that the humanist outlook can provide the moral basis for a world-wide mission for the safety of unborn generations. Humanists usually profess a kind of utilitarianism which seeks the greatest happiness of the greatest number; and, since the greatest number of people probably belong to posterity rather than the present, those who profess this ethic might seem to owe a duty towards people of the future. But the basis of utilitarianism is enlightened self-interest, and so it does not seem to be applicable to the unknown future.

Humanists have been attempting lately to provide a reasoned alternative to theistic belief which does justice to human values, and a collection of essays has recently been published entitled *The Humanist Outlook* (edited by A. J. Ayer, Pemberton, London, 1968). In the introduction (p. 6) Professor Ayer points out that, if capacity for evil is part of human nature, so also is capacity for good. This seems obvious enough, but it does not resolve the problems of posterity. Professor Ginsberg holds that the balance of evidence is on the side of moral progress (p. 141), and he may well be right. However he instances it by drawing attention to the 'growing recognition of a duty to posterity' (p. 142). But he gives no evidence for this other than 'the importance attached to the study of population problems'. Recognition of a problem, alas, is quite different from acceptance of a moral imperative. Kingsley Martin in his contribution averred that each one of us must decide for himself what ends he thinks

47

it right to pursue and what principles he is prepared to stand by; and Professor Ayer adds that there is no escaping this responsibility (p. 7). But posterity depends on our acceptance of a *universal* duty towards future generations and our willingness to act on this obligation. This weakness in the humanist position appears clearly in the contribution of Lord Ritchie-Calder who has shown such practical and praiseworthy concern for posterity and whose writings have been appreciatively cited in these lectures. Lord Ritchie-Calder is full of zeal to help posterity, but when it comes to moral obligation he contents himself with mere assertion. 'In humanist ethics we should accept the trusteeship for future generations' (p. 160). Excellent; but *why*? And what difference will this make? The future of mankind can only be assured by a *universal* willingness to undertake such trusteeship rather than its inclusion within the ethics of those humanists who happen to decide that way.

In one recent humanist exposition there has been no attempt to apply ethics at all to this problem. Dr Edmund Leach's Reith Lectures for 1967, published under the title *A Runaway World?*, show only too clearly the hollowness of his humanist position. In his first lecture the Provost of King's College, Cambridge, poses his question as follows:[11]
Men have become like gods. Isn't it about time that we understood our divinity? Science offers us total mastery over our environment and over our destiny, yet instead of rejoicing we are deeply afraid. Why should this be? How might these fears be resolved?

Dr Leach very properly castigates scientists for trying to opt

48

out of tough decisions. *Laisser-faire* will not do. He insists that the right decisions must be taken by people properly equipped to take them:

We simply must take charge of our own fate. We must somehow see to it that the decisions which have long-term consequences are taken by men who understand what they are doing and not by bewildered amateurs. And it could be so. Change need not always be something that happens to us: it could be something which we choose to bring about.[12]

Dr Leach then goes on to discuss the consequences of such participation. It is here that he introduces obliquely the motives behind such action:

By participating in history instead of standing by to watch we shall at least be able to enjoy the present. The cult of scientific detachment and the orderly fragmented way of living that goes with it, serve only to isolate the human individual from his environment and from his neighbours – they reduce him to a lonely, impotent and terrified observer of a runaway world. A more positive attitude to change will not mean that you will always feel more secure, it will just give you a sense of purpose. You should read your Homer. Gods who manipulate the course of history are no more likely to achieve their private ambitions than are men who suffer the slings and arrows of outrageous fortune; but gods have much more fun![13]

'It will just give you a sense of purpose.' 'Gods have much more fun.' Those are the reasons that Dr Leach gives for our concern for posterity. *What* sense of purpose? Is taking thought for tomorrow simply a way of giving people (and necessarily only a few people) that sense of purpose for which their psyche craves? Is it simply a way for them to have fun? I am sure that Dr Leach in fact believes that it is much more than that, but I do not see how, in terms of the humanism that he professes, concern for posterity could logically be put into ethical terms. I have dealt with these Reith Lectures in some detail because of the great popular interest which they aroused. I cannot believe that the reasons which Dr Leach gave for intelligent participation in change for the sake of posterity are likely to stir sufficiently men's will and imagination to co-operate in making the colossal effort of self-restraint that seems required.

What will be sufficient for this? Until men come to believe in their hearts that all life is held in trust from God, there can be no valid ethical reason why we should owe a duty to posterity. Once it is believed that men hold their dominion over all nature as stewards and trustees for God, then immediately they are confronted by an inalienable duty towards and concern for their total environment, present and future; and this duty towards environment does not merely include their fellow-men, but all nature and all life.

This has the most momentous consequences. From the last lecture it seemed to be clear that if man is not by his folly, frailty and ignorance to ruin his environment and with it his own future, then the most tremendous and unprecedented efforts to prevent this will be necessary. Plainly man must have a sufficient motive force to inspire his imagination and to fire his will to co-operate in such an enterprise. I have suggested that this can only come about through a lively belief in God as the Creator whose Spirit animates and energises the cosmos. From this flows man's conviction of his status as God's steward.

Please note that I have not said anything specifically Christian at this point. It is something on which Jews, Muslims, Hindus and theistic Buddhists would all agree. Christians ought surely to be glad that they share with those of other faiths such fundamental convictions. Logically we are forced to a strange (and to some perhaps unpalatable) conclusion. Theistic religion, far from being outmoded in these days of science and technology, appears the only hope of a world endangered by science and technology. Belief in man's creatureliness and in his accountability before God seem literally essential for the future salvation of this planet. This was the burden of the prophets' message to Israel. The situation now has changed, and it is not just Israel's accountability that now matters, nor just that of the Church as the 'Israel of God', but the accountability of the whole human race. In this universal context the prophets' words are still supremely relevant. 'Seek ye the Lord while he may be found, call ye upon him while he is near . . . let him return unto the Lord, and he will have mercy upon him.'[14] 'Return, O backsliding children.'[15] 'For thus saith the Lord unto the house of Israel, Seek ye me, and ye shall live.'[16] These verses, in the light of our environmental future, have a terrible and immediate relevance. Just as some of the Visions of the End (such as the Seven Plagues of Wrath in Revelation 16) seem to have a remarkable similarity to possible future disasters, so the prophets' insistence that natural catastrophies will follow disobedience to God seem particularly applicable today.

But we must not be *simpliste*. Mere belief in God will not get anybody anywhere. Mere repentance, in the sense of turning our backs on past disbelief, will not bring safety to posterity. The problems facing humanity need clear analysis before any way forward can be seen. All that realization of our accountability before God can give us is the moral and spiritual determination to co-operate in making this planet safe for ourselves and posterity: it cannot by itself achieve that safety. The very fact that *mankind* is accountable means that *mankind* has to work out its own salvation in fear and trembling.

An analysis of the reasons why mankind is in its present situation we shall consider later. First let us consider what it means to say that man is God's steward over nature.

We turn here to the Bible. It may seem that the Bible has been brought rather late into this discussion. But this is not so. The Bible is not to be used as a kind of infallible tourists' guide book to life, written on an overall plan by a single hand. It is rather a unique and inspired collection of sacred writings, Jewish and Christian, with books of varying value and amazing insights. One of these insights is that man is made in the image of God. 'And God said, Let us make man in our image, after our likeness: and let them have dominion over the fish of the sea, and over the fowl of the air, and over the cattle, and over all the earth, and over every creeping thing that creepeth upon the earth. And God created man in his own image, in the image of God created he him; male and female created he them.'[17] Whatever else it may mean to be in God's image, here it is connected with universal dominion and sexual differentiation. Man is vice-regent for God. As the Psalmist says of man: 'Thou hast made him but little lower than God, and crownest him with glory and honour. Thou madest him to have dominion over the works of thy hands; thou has put all things under his feet.'[18] And, as the author of the Epistle to the Hebrews comments on the verse, 'in that he subjected all things unto him, he left nothing that is not subject to him'. When the Epistle was written that was true in principle: but soon, with man's increasing mastery over his environment, it will be true also in practice.

This dominion of man over nature means that he must act as God's viceregent, that is to say, he must exercise his powers in accordance with God's moral nature. His sense of responsibility, no less than his status in creation, must be little less than God's.[19] Man not only has dominion over nature, but he is part of nature, according to the biblical picture. He is made of the dust of the earth,[20] and the future of man is seen in close connection with the future of nature.[21]

The account in Genesis of man's dominion is also coupled with the command to be fruitful and multiply. 'And God blessed them: and God said unto them, Be fruitful, and multiply, and replenish the earth, and subdue it; and have dominion over the fish of the sea, and over the fowl of the air, and over every living thing that moveth upon the earth.'[22] This verse has often been used as a kind of proof-text to permit wanton destruction of the animal and vegetable kingdoms and to license unlimited human procreation within the institution of marriage. To draw either of these conclusions from this verse is an abuse of scriptural exegesis. Man has dominion over nature, yes; but to exercise that dominion in a way which is wanton and cruel is as sinful for man as it is alien to the nature of God. Man, because he is made in God's image, is a moral being, accountable to God for his actions; and because he is made in the image of God, man is also an intelligent being, under an obligation to use his mind in the exercise of his dominion and therefore unjustified in abusing his environment through indifference or lack of forethought. So far as human reproduction is concerned, the passage contains a blessing on fertility and an injunction to fill the earth. It does not contain an injunction to overflow and overfill the earth. The historical context of the Genesis story must be realized. It was written when the population of the world was small and the life of man was short and uncertain. There was a vast and apparently unlimited amount of *Lebensraum* for man's expanding population, and a multitude of wild beasts to subdue. The idea of world overpopulation would have seemed fantastic to its author. In any case the command is to multiply, not to go on multiplying *ad infinitum*.

So man must exercise his dominion responsibly. But what has gone wrong? Why is there a danger that his dominion will get out of control?

The traditional Christian explanation has been that man has inherited original sin from his first ancestor Adam, and because of this he cannot fail in his unregenerate state to do wrong. The Thirty-nine Articles of the Church of England are no longer, thank goodness, the test of Anglican ortho-doxy, and it will be convenient to cite from them the opening words of Article IX which sum up well the tradi-tional Christian viewpoint:

Original Sin standeth not in the following of *Adam*, (as the *Pelagians* do vainly talk;) but it is the fault and corruption of the Nature of every man, that naturally is ingendered of the offspring of *Adam*; whereby man is very far gone from original righteous-ness, and is of his own nature inclined to evil, so that the flesh lusteth always contrary to the spirit; and therefore in every person born into this world, it deserveth God's wrath and damnation.

This has worn a bit threadbare today! There is no doubt that we sin: there is no doubt that we behave other than we wish and other than we ought, both as individuals and as groups. But it is altogether *simpliste* to put this down merely to Adam, however much we may be determined by our genetic inheritance. Our self-knowledge, helped by the researches of zoologists, anthropologists, sociologists, psychologists and even anatomists, tells us that there is more to it than just that.

As a result of these researches, we are now able to see man far more easily as part of nature as well as a unique species within nature. The story of evolution from hydrogen atoms in a formless cosmos to human beings with all their talents and potentialities, is not yet complete. But the gaps are not large, and the main picture is easily discernible; and happily this process of evolution is no longer seen to be incompatible with the Christian faith.[23] The study of wild

animals, and particularly mammals, has been of special
interest because the instinctive reactions of these animals in
their natural state have shed much light on human behaviour.
All the main animal drives of grooming, sex, rearing,
exploration, feeding and aggression normally find expression
in *Homo sapiens*.[24] Even self-consciousness, which had
previously been associated with man alone among living
beings, is now seen to be present, albeit in a rather different
form, among animals.[25] Animals are innocent, in as much
as they have no moral consciousness. Human beings, however, are capable of free choice and moral sensibility, and
thus responsible for their actions. Indeed this is one of the
reasons why they can be said to be in the image of God.
Man differs from the animals not merely in possessing moral
consciousness, but also in an abnormally long childhood,
with the result that childhood experiences of frustration and
dependence seem to influence him all his life, and endow
him with tragic potentialities which can turn aggression into
hate. Man also has the power to abstract himself from his
surroundings, and so to withdraw from reality into a dream
world of his own, where he can indulge in fantasies of his
enemies' hatred. Man seems, in the phrase of Lorenz, rather
like a dove who has acquired the beak of a raven. 'All his
troubles arise from his being a basically harmless, omnivorous creature, lacking in natural weapons with which to
kill big prey, and, therefore, devoid of the built-in safety
devices which prevent "professional" carnivores from
abusing their killing power to destroy fellow members of
their own species.'[26] These natural weapons seem to have

been used by the forebears of *Homo sapiens* to achieve dominance over other species.[27] The fact that nowadays weapons in modern warfare are rarely those of personal combat depersonalises the foe and so increases the dangers of man's aggressive drives. 'Man is a competitive, aggressive, territorial animal. He is also a social animal who needs the support of others of his own kind and opponents from whom he can distinguish himself in order to affirm his own sense of identity.'[28]

Not all ethologists would agree with such a view of aggression; and indeed the very word needs further definition before it can be precisely described. The view of Lorenz, Ardrey and Storr that aggression is a genetically inherited spontaneous drive has been hotly contested.[29] Their arguments are said to suffer from neglect of experience, selective evidence and misinterpretation of fact.[30] Into such a technical debate it ill becomes an amateur to enter; but in any case the argument seems for our purposes to be rather 'academic'. For even if aggression could be demonstrated not to be spontaneous, it would still be shown to be aroused by such stimulae as pain, proximity or frustration. As these, alas, seem endemic in our human situation, aggression remains a natural and inevitable factor in human life.

Thus both aggressiveness and a drive towards integration are natural to man's condition, and neither in itself is either good or bad. It is particularly dangerous to repress aggressiveness. 'If society is in danger, it is not because of man's aggressiveness but because of the repression of personal aggressiveness in individuals.'[31] Without aggressiveness, man would never have 'attacked problems' or 'got his teeth into' obstacles or 'overcome' difficulties or 'mastered' a situation.[32] Yet, without a drive towards integration, men would never have been able to combine together and pool their efforts and find community and fellowship.

All these entails from man's animal past, together with his own human *differentiae*, may be called 'original sin' if it is found helpful to retain the phrase.

Aggression is only one of man's drives, a dangerous one in view of man's paranoid tendencies to turn aggression into hatred. Man is unlike most mammals, who, instead of fighting to the death, usually reduce interspecific conflict to display.[33] But Koestler is surely right in pointing out that aggression is not the most dangerous instinct. 'The main danger lies precisely in what we are wont to call his "better nature"... *the integrative tendencies of the individual are incomparably more dangerous than his self-assertive tendencies*. The sermons of the reformers were bound to fall on deaf ears because they put the blame where it did not belong.'[34] Koestler goes on to claim that 'crimes of violence committed for selfish, personal motives are historically insignificant compared to those committed *ad majorem gloriam Dei*, out of a self-sacrificing devotion to a flag, a leader, a religious faith or a political conviction'.[35] On the one hand aggression has been the cause of man's greatest achievements as well as his basest actions, and on the other hand 'the glory and the tragedy of the human condition *both derive from our powers of self-transcendence*'.[36] Only when self-assertion is mixed with self-transcending tendencies can human nature reach its full maturity. But both can also be fused together to raise hell upon earth. War, for example, is the result of man's self-transcending identification with a cause which results in the unleashing of his aggressive self-assertion.

Koestler, discussing the causes of man's predicament, believes that man has a mentality split between faith and reason, emotion and intellect.[37] 'The delusional streak running through history is not due to individual forms of lunacy, but to the collective delusions generated by emotion-based belief-systems . . . . the cause underlying these pathological manifestations is the split between reason and belief – or more generally, insufficient co-ordination between the emotive and discriminative faculties of the mind.'[38] And Koestler, when he goes on to ask the cause of this capacity for delusion, answers it anatomically. Man, he says, is a biological freak, the result of some remarkable mistake in the evolutionary process. He cites Le Gros Clark as saying that 'the rapidity of the evolutionary expansion of the brain during the Pleistocene is an example of what has been termed "explosive evolution"'.[39] It has long been realised that the cause of many psychosomatic and psychoneurotic diseases is the lack of co-ordination between the higher centres of the brain and the diencephalon.[40] Koestler, drawing on later cortical discoveries, believes that the dissonant functioning of the 'old' and 'new' parts of our brains has built 'schizophysiology' into our species, resulting in the delusional streak which runs through human history.

This may all be too true. The Genesis stories of original sin are attempts to explain mythologically a basic fault in human nature. I have sketched in earlier in this lecture possible psychological and, so to say, zoological explanations. Presumably there is an anatomical counterpart, and for all I know Koestler may have hit upon it.[41] But his solution appals me. He hopes for a mental stabiliser, perhaps a synthetic hormone which will correct this delusional streak, inserted into water supplies like common chlorine. The outcry against fluoride suggests that this is a non-starter; but in any case to do this would be to dehumanise man. We are what we are, for better or for worse: and Koestler has not proved that it *may* not be for better, only that in the past it has often been for worse.

It may properly be claimed that only a religion can harness both the integrative and the aggressive drives of mankind. Must all religions cause collective delusions? Can these drives be directed into constructive and creative channels? We have already noted that the only hope for mankind seems to lie in faith in God. What is needed, therefore, is a theistic religion which does not involve its adherents in fanatical devotion but which inspires them to co-operation with all men within a competitive framework. We need a religion which is not exclusive in the sense that it denies the worth of all other religions and belief-systems or denigrates all non-adherents, but which is unique in the sense that its institutional structure only exists to serve the needs of others. I suggest that what is required not only on the grounds of truth but also on the grounds of world need is a reformed, remythologised and revitalised Christianity.

Now I have spent so much time in this lecture on attempting to analyse the natural deficiencies of *Homo sapiens* because the environmental crisis in which we shall shortly find ourselves is not due to outward factors so much as to the drives within man which are the root cause of the crisis. To take steps now to deal only with the environment would be to treat only the symptoms of what is wrong. No doubt in emergency symptoms do need treatment. But the symptoms will simply recur unless they are dealt with at the roots.

Let us therefore return to the environmental crisis which I tried to analyse and explain in the first lecture. What are the root causes of this crisis?

First comes the size of the problem. Earlier in the planet's history groups could not inflict damage on those who lived far distant from them. Now, however, owing to the magnitude of man's activities, we are one world. World-wide co-operation in control of our environment is becoming essential to world survival. Man's greatest problem is now not merely social, but world-wide. This means that not merely co-existence is essential but full interstate co-operation. Some system must be evolved which harnesses man's integrative drives for such co-operation without submerging the needs of the individual. Is such a system possible?

Secondly comes overpopulation, causing strain on food supplies, and social stress which is resulting in psychological imbalance and in particular increased aggressive drives. The increased population also results in greater production and so the degree and rate of ecological pollution is accelerated.

Whatever else happens, the population of the world needs to be brought to a level which reduces psychological strain and physical malnutrition. Is such a reduction possible? Even if the technical means were universally available, would men and women avail themselves of it?

Thirdly, there must be *knowledge* of the crisis that imperils man's future. This means both research in ecology and in the particular disciplines under which our various environmental problems should be classified. Much more than research is needed, of course. People must *know* about these dangers; not just scientists, not just statesmen, but ordinary people, the kind of people who will actually be affected, either in their own lifetime or in the lifetime of their posterity. No one can be expected to exercise self-control on behalf of posterity without an awareness that such action is absolutely essential for their survival and well-being, particularly as the dangers are not yet obvious. Is such self-control possible, even granting that the facts are known?

Fourthly, countries must agree together on a ceiling to the material standard of living that is possible if we are to keep some kind of ecological balance which is compatible with the well-being of the human species. How could this agreement possibly be reached without a renewal of our eschatological hope? Gross inequalities would be intolerable if a ceiling were to be placed on the world's material standard of living, and so it would become necessary for developed countries to cry halt to their search for ever higher standards of living. Is this possible? Is it possible to create renewed respect for the inexorable working of natural law? Ecological balance is a necessity of the natural law, and imbalance inevitably has dire results for man who is completely dependent on the functioning of his ecosystems.

It is unfortunate that one single aspect of human ecology, such as artificial birth-control, should have been singled out as contrary to natural law. In one sense contraception is contrary to natural law, since it prohibits or inhibits the natural function of human reproduction. On the other hand in any such appraisal artificial birth-control should not be considered in its moral aspect separately from artificial death-control, artificial pollution of the environment, or artificial technological developments that result in the plundering of natural resources. Life is complex and finely balanced, and any pronouncement about the natural law must take note of this complexity and balance.

Fifthly, steps must be taken to see that the natural instinctive drives of men can have healthy and creative outlets. Can this be done? I have suggested that the integrative tendencies in man can only find their proper and harmonious fulfilment in the worship of God. Today they are distorted so that men identify themselves not with God but with a particular religion or ideology or patriotism, or men attempt to create self-transcendence by simulated mystical experience, induced by drugs. I have argued that man's only hope is renewed belief in God before whom he is accountable as steward and trustee. I have suggested that our integrative tendencies can only be fully and harmoniously satisfied by faith in a loving, purposeful Creator whose Spirit vitalises and energises the universe and who cares for individual people who have emerged within the evolutionary process within which his Spirit is at work.

But what of the other drives in man's nature? We may say that today his grooming instincts drive man towards ever higher material standards of comfort; feeding instincts lead man towards obesity when there is an abundance of food to tempt him; aggressive instincts, stimulated by social stress, tend to result in hatred and delinquency; sexual instincts tend towards promiscuity and perversion in a society made sick through rapid urbanisation and social change; rearing instincts tend to be twisted and frustrated in modern cultures so that psychological imbalance is often irremediably created in infancy and early childhood; exploration instincts are given free rein in a world so intent on technological progress that it gives no thought for the biological consequences of new discoveries. Can these instincts be channelled into healthy and creative channels? Have they not become as dangerous as man's integrative tendencies?

One step at a time. In the first lecture I tried to state the problem. In this lecture I have argued that our only hope lies in renewed faith in God. In the last lecture I turn to the particular contribution of the Christian faith.

Lecture delivered 28 January 1969, under the title 'The Future of Humanity'.

Lecture Three

CHRISTIANITY AND THE FUTURE

According to a long-standing Christian tradition, there are three (so-called) theological virtues; faith, hope and charity. Christians have faith in the loving purposes of God on the grounds of what he did in the past through Christ, charity towards all men in response to God's charity towards mankind, and hope – what is Christian hope? Is it some woolly optimism about something we don't know, or a facile expectation of future wish fulfilment? There is, I think, more confusion over the theological virtue of hope than almost any other Christian doctrine, and that is saying a very great deal.

The clearest statement that I have ever seen of what people used to believe was given by J. S. Bezzant in his lecture on 'Intellectual Objections' in *Objections to Christian Belief*.[1]

It began with an alleged rebellion of Satan against God in which angels fell. By direct acts of God, Adam and Eve were created, apparently as adults, not only innocent but fully righteous. Their descendants were intended to restore the number of the angels depleted by the heavenly revolt. Moved by envy, Satan persuaded our first parents to disobey one absolute command of God, that they were not to obtain knowledge, and so brought about their fall from original righteousness, in consequence of which they transmitted to all their offspring, by natural generation, a corrupted nature wholly inclined to evil, an enfeebled will, and also the guilt of their sin. Thus all mankind lay under the curse of sin both original and actual, the object of divine wrath and destined to damnation. In order to restore his thwarted purpose God sent his Son who, assuming human nature, was born on earth, whereon was wrought the drama of his death and resurrection. Jesus, pure from all defect of original and actual sin, alone fulfilled the conditions of a perfect sacrifice for human sin. By this God's legitimate anger with guilty mankind was appeased and his honour satisfied; he was graciously pleased to accept his Son's sacrifice, enabled to forgive sin, and man was potentially redeemed. The Christian church, a Divine corporation, came into being; those baptised into it who by grace persevered in the fulfilment of its commands would be secure in the life to come. From the supernatural life of the church, the world and history derived their meaning and without it would at a last day perish by fire. This would happen when the unknown number of souls required to replace the fallen angels was complete. The Anglican Prayerbook office for the burial of the dead still prays that God may be pleased shortly to accomplish the number of the elect and to hasten his kingdom. The dead would be raised from their graves in their bodies, despite St. Paul's clear assertion that flesh and blood cannot inherit the kingdom of God nor corruption incorruption. The saved were predestined to their salvation by an inscrutable decree of God, not for any merits of their own but solely for those of Christ. As to the fate of the rest, there were differences of opinion, but it was generally held that they would suffer endless torments in the flames of a hell, by which climax not only would God's power and justice be finally vindicated but heaven's bliss intensified.

This may sound like a travesty, but in fact it is a very fair statement of medieval orthodoxy. This is what Christian hope used to mean. The medieval scheme of salvation sounds today like the reasoning of diseased minds pathologically disturbed by guilt and fear. The medieval view was not the same as the New Testament teaching. It was however sufficiently close to it to find some support from the pages of the Bible.

The Bible itself does not give a clear and unequivocal account of the Christian scheme of salvation. We look to it not for a blueprint but for inspired insights. In the New Testament there are varying accounts and varying interpretations of the coming of Christ, divergent in some respects but all agreeing in their acknowledgement of him as Lord. These biblical differences show that there is room for divergences in the interpretation of the Christian faith in every age. If we reject today the medieval scheme of salvation as unworthy of God, this does not mean that we can go back to the interpretation which we find in Holy Scripture. Indeed this is impossible, for as we have already noted there is no single biblical *doctrine* of salvation. There are in the Bible various *doctrines* of salvation, and we have no clear criterion by which we can make one more normative than another. Any modern interpretation must, of course, seek to understand the biblical doctrines, for the Bible is inspired in its witness to the activity of God, particularly in Jesus Christ, and for its illuminating insights into truth.

67

Again and again the Bible raises fundamental questions of ultimate concern to every age. But each age must take account of the full sum of truth as known to it in seeking a contemporary interpretation of the Christian faith.

Any such modern account must take into consideration our natural and social sciences which have enabled us to understand so much of God's activity within his universe. We now have a vision of the kind of way in which the world evolved under the influence of God's spirit moving within it; about the way in which *Homo sapiens* evolved and gained dominance over nature; about the way in which man's instincts have evolved, his brain has enlarged and his capacity for ratiocination and personal relationships has grown. We can even trace the way in which his moral consciousness has emerged and his religious beliefs have taken shape and become articulated. All this the man of faith can see as the result of God's creative spirit working within his created universe. The result is to give a meaning for life, a standard for behaviour and a living relationship and communion with God, both for individuals and for social groups. God discloses himself in many ways and among all people, but he set aside the Jews to serve his purposes and to reveal his righteousness; and in particular he prepared the way for his personal self-disclosure in Jesus of Nazareth. Here God disclosed his own nature to men, and here also man can see a total human response to God in the human terms which alone he can understand. The humbleness and acceptance by Jesus of his fate disclose in particular God's total acceptance of man despite his failures and follies and all his feelings of inadequacy.[2] Man is therefore helped to accept himself, and growth towards full maturity becomes at last a real possibility. Furthermore, Jesus' uncompromising stand for truth discloses both the mind of God and man's response, so that the Christian is under an obligation to use his gifts of intelligence as rigorously and honestly as he can.

Why did God create? Creation in one sense is an 'unnecessary' act of God, in as much as he cannot 'need' human companionship. On the other hand it is a 'necessity' of love to be self-giving, and God may be presumed to have created the universe at least in part so that beings could evolve capable of exercising free choice and of entering into personal relationships with him. This leads to the presumption that God did not as it were wish to keep his blessings to himself, but desires men to share these with him, and to 'enter into the joy of their Lord'. The ultimate goal of man is therefore to enjoy God for ever. This life is the first chapter in a pilgrimage the length of which and the details of which are unknown to us; and so too are the other purposes which God may or may not have in creating and sustaining our evolving cosmos.

If this be true, the ultimate goal of men is to share together and for ever in the blessing of God; to be with him and to enjoy him for eternity. What then of the future of this earth? It is to be valued both for its own sake, and in the light of our final goal. Men must strive to see that justice and righteousness flourish as much as possible, because these are the will of God and without them it is not possible to live in true community. A sufficient standard of living is also necessary to enable human character to mature sufficiently that it may hereafter flower and bear fruit. The aim of social and political ambitions should be to produce the conditions under which all men can realise their potentialities both as individuals and as members of a community. The role of the Church is not to be 'triumphal', lording it over the secular world, but rather to be 'the servant Church', serving with humbleness the true needs of the world, attending to its primary task of worship and acting as a means of grace through which men are enabled to accept their frailties and limitations, and where they can find freedom from bondage to their past. The function of a Church in a dehumanised society is to provide for men some means of self-identity and to humanise sterile and impersonal institutions. The past history of Christendom does not give ground for hope that the Church in itself is likely to help men and women in the resolution of their problems; but the Church would seem, humanly speaking, to be essential for the renewal of men and women who can then in practical ways apply their minds personally and politically and socially to the re-ordering of society. The role of the Church is not to attempt to solve the problems which beset the future of *Homo sapiens*, but to provide the inspiration and the insights with which men and women who have the requisite secular skills and knowledge may resolve them.

If this short summary of a modern Christian scheme of salvation be anywhere near the mark, certain conclusions relevant to the theme of these lectures seem to emerge.

In the first place, eternity is man's ultimate goal, and the main function of our present life is not merely its enjoyment, so far as possible for its own sake, but also growth in character, by means of the material conditions of life, so that men may be better able to reach their final goal beyond this life.[3] Without this eternal perspective it is impossible to get right our priorities in this world. The secular is not diminished in importance. On the contrary it is the only means whereby we can be in communion with God in this world, and it is the only means whereby men can grow into maturity and so be made ready for eternal life. This perspective of eternity gives heightened importance to and thus heightened concern for the affairs of this world. 'The Saints' Everlasting Rest' may sometimes be used as an escape from the ugly realities of this world. But it should be not only the inspiration behind individual spirituality but also the stimulus behind legislative reform, social endeavour and political action. Seen in this light, this world becomes not merely an end in itself but a preparation for a larger and more final goal. To deny this larger goal, or to ignore its importance is to pervert a true perspective. It is the *trahison des clercs* of the twentieth century.

Some explanation is needed to understand how this false perspective has come about. Strangely enough it is bound up with a renewal of interest in the doctrine about the last things, called in ecclesiastical jargon 'eschatology'. 'Christian eschatology,' wrote the Bishop of Woolwich, 'is neither a tentative guess at how in distant ages the evolutionary process may work out; nor is it a specific programme of immediate catastrophe. It is the lighting up of a new dimension of life *now*.'[4] It is not difficult to see where this kind of thinking leads. On the one hand Christian theology has become so Christocentric that it ignores the realities of this world. A recent book on Christian hope, hailed by German theologians as the work of a brilliant mind, contains these word: 'Christian eschatology does not speak of the future as such . . . . Christian eschatology speaks of Jesus and *his* future. . . . The question whether all statements about the future are grounded in the person and history of Jesus Christ provides it with the touchstone by which to distinguish the spirit of eschatology from that of utopia.'[5] On the other hand, other modern theologians refuse to think in futurist terms at all. For many thinkers eschatology has become merely a kind of added dimension given to present existence. Many younger theologians seem to be almost intoxicated by the secular, and appear to be uninterested in or deny 'the life of the world to come', in contrast to older Christian thinkers such as Reinhold Niebuhr,[6] E. Brunner,[7] and J. E. Fison,[8] who have kept a more balanced perspective. Some recent books best illustrate the point. Macquarrie, in *God and Secularity* does not even mention eternal life and can say nothing more of Christian hope than that 'nothing can be so mean or "profane", nothing even can be so wicked, that it cannot somehow be worked upon by God's redemptive and creative love and that it cannot finally serve his purpose'.[9] J. J. Vincent in a recent book called *The Secular Christ*, can say no more of the gift of eternal life than that it is 'the gift of ultimate significance'.[10] Harvey Cox speaks of the secular city as the best image by which to understand what the New Testament writers called the Kingdom of God.[11] (This is in contrast to Lord Ritchie-Calder who has called the city of the future 'Hell upon Earth'.) Harvey Cox seems to believe that repentance means merely laying aside previous values and loyalties, and freely entering the new reality.[12] This seems to approach by another route the Utopianism of earlier liberal thought, and the Archbishop of Canterbury, in a recent book, has commented: 'With all his insights Harvey Cox is only misleading if he diverts from this: "Woe is me, for I am lost, . . . for my eyes have seen the King, the Lord of hosts".'[13]

I have called the loss of our eternal perspective our contemporary *trahison des clercs* because it is not only wrong in itself, but also it does nothing to challenge the contemporary *laisser-faire* in scientific and technological development which is raising a question mark over the very future of man himself. If there is no perspective of eternity, man is bound to exploit this world to the full, and he will find good reasons for attempting an ever higher material standard of living in the secular city. Only the perspective of eternity, combined with a heartfelt conviction of man's accountability before God, is likely to modify this self-defeating aim. The East has a tradition of ignoring this world, and the West of concentrating on this world alone. Both have much to learn from each other. A proper perspective is essential.

If my first point concerns eternal life, my second is the illusory hope of a worldly Utopia. Indeed, the burden of the prophets' message in the Old Testament is the imminent

73

destruction of the known world-order, and in the New Testament the early expectation of the world's end is taken for granted, and the delay in its denouement provided a puzzle for many. In one sense the Kingdom came through Jesus, and individuals may enter it now; but, it is always God's gift, and if it is ever to be fulfilled on earth, it could never come through man's efforts but by the cataclysmic intrusion of God. Man can never perfect himself or his society. Science has further filled in the biblical picture. Medawar, in his Reith Lectures,[14] said of man's perfectibility:

There seems no doubt that some large part of human fitness is vested in a mechanism which provides for a high degree of genetic inequality and inborn diversity, which makes sure that there are plenty of different kinds of human beings; and this fact sets a limit to any purely theoretical fancies we may care to indulge in about the perfectibility of men.

(This does not of course mean that man is incapable of further genetical improvement. If it is true that man carries a number of inactive or 'nonsense' genes, it is possible that he has a reserve of unused capacity so that in appropriate circumstances he may continue to evolve.)[15] Whatever be the possibilities of growth on this planet towards perfectibility, its eventual future seems not to be in doubt. The Kingdom of God can never fully come in this world-order. The final destiny of our planet has been well put by Professor Fred Hoyle in his famous lectures published under the title *The Nature of the Universe*. He said:

The Sun will grow steadily more luminous as its hydrogen supply is converted into helium, and this will go on until the oceans boil on the Earth. . . . as the Sun grills the Earth it will swell, at first slowly and then with increasing rapidity until it swallows the inner planets . . .[16]

This fate is still some time off, of course, probably some 10,000,000,000 years ahead,[17] but whether it happens sooner or later, it points to the transitoriness of human society.

It is not necessary however to look as far ahead as that. It is possible to consider merely the future of man:

Biologists do not agree about the mechanism of the continual disappearance of phyla in the course of geological time, a process almost as mysterious as that of their formation; but the reality of the phenomenon is indisputable. . . . The days (or the millennia) of every living form are by statistical reckoning ineluctably numbered; so much so that, using the scale of time furnished by the study of certain isotopes, it is beginning to be possible to calculate in millions of years *the average life of a species*.[18]

Teilhard de Chardin goes on to comment: 'Man now sees that the seeds of his ultimate dissolution are at the heart of his being. The *End of the Species* is in the marrow of our bones!'[19] And yet this is not really what he believes. He held that man is an exception, and denied that man's future is circumscribed like that of other species:

For if by its structure Mankind does not dissipate itself but concentrates upon itself; in other words, if, alone among all the living forms known to us, our zoological phylum is laboriously moving towards a *critical point of speciation*, then are not all hopes permitted to us in the matter of survival and irreversibility?

The end of a 'thinking species': not disintegration and death, but a new break-through and a re-birth, this time outside Time and Space, through the very excess of unification and co-reflexion.[20]

Teilhard is such a big thinker that it is unfair to quote a single sentence. Elsewhere he wrote:

The more we study the past, noting the steady rise of Life over millions of years, and observing the ever-growing multitude of reflective elements engaged in the construction of the Noosphere; the more must we be convinced that by a sort of 'infallibility of large numbers' Mankind, the present crest of the evolutionary wave, cannot fail in the course of its guided probings to find the right road and an outlet for its higher ascent. . . . It is reasoned calculation, not speculation, which makes me ready to lay odds on the ultimate triumph of hominisation over all the vicissitudes threatening its progress.[21]

Teilhard de Chardin, if I may be permitted to speak thus of a great Christian and a truly brilliant scientific pioneer,[22] seems to me seriously to undervalue the power of sin, frailty and evil in the world. In the collected papers published under the title *The Future of Man* sin is not mentioned in the index, and as for evil, he is only prepared to see this as apparent disaster in a process of liberation.[23] I wonder if he would have written thus if he had realised the coming environmental crisis for man? It seems as though Teilhard was really writing out of speculative faith rather than reasoned calculation. Moreover I wonder why such a belief should be for him a certainty of faith. It was not so for Jesus, who, whatever were his precise beliefs about the last things, surely shared with his contemporaries faith in the coming end of this world-order. And I do not see why the guarantee of man's future need be a certainty of faith for us. Sometimes Teilhard speculates in a mystic vein which seems to suggest that he sees the way ahead for man in a purely spiritual mode. He wonders whether mankind, 'leaving Earth and stars to lapse slowly back into the dwindling mass of primordial energy, . . . will detach itself from this planet and join the one true, irreversible essence of things, the Omega point'.[24] By then man would have ceased to be man at all.

The first point I have made concerns eternal life, and the second the futility of an earthly Utopia. I next want to assert the importance of the secular. 'The Word became flesh and dwelt among us', and so the material and the secular became the vehicle and mode of God's self-disclosure. I suppose that it is Teilhard again who has re-awakened us to a fresh vision of this truth today. The secular is the field of God's self-disclosure and activity. If we have needed Teilhard to remind us of this great truth, others in their day and in their way knew this as well as he. Take for example some lines from Pope's *Essay on Man* on this great theme:[25]

> All are but parts of one stupendous whole
> Whose body Nature is, and God the soul;
> That, chang'd through all, and yet in all the same,
> Great in the earth, as in th' æthereal frame,
> Warms in the sun, refreshes in the breeze,
> Glows in the stars, and blossoms in the trees;
> Lives through all life, extends through all extent,
> Spreads undivided, operates unspent;
> Breathes in our soul, informs our mortal part,
> As full, as perfect, in a hair as heart;
> As full, as perfect, in vile man that mourns

77

As the rapt Seraph that adores and burns:
To him no high, no low, no great, no small;
He fills, he bounds, connects, and equals all.

If the secular is the medium and mode of God's activity and self-disclosure, then we must look to the secular as well as to the spiritual for the solution of many of our problems concerning our environment. Let me illustrate my point.

I ended my second lecture by attempting to analyse the various root-causes of the difficulties that beset man's future. The first concerned the size of the problem. I said that some system must be evolved which gives men the will to co-operate, a system that harnesses man's integrative drives without submerging the needs of the individual. In part this poses a religious and spiritual problem. Can a religious faith give men such a feeling of universal brother-hood that they will be willing to co-operate, if only for the survival of the species? I suggested that a remythologised and revitalised Christianity could do this. But the problem is not merely religious: it is also secular. Co-operation on a world-wide scale needs great expertise in modern technology and in modern communications. These are secular skills, involving diplomacy, international co-operation and ad-ministration, and economic controls. Without these skills, co-operation in the modern world becomes impossible.

The second cause of danger is so well known that little need be said here. Overpopulation threatens man through insufficiency of living space and of sustenance. The resolution of this problem is partly a technical one. Agricultural sciences and skills have a part to play, as well as conservation techniques, in the production of food. City-planning can reduce the dangers of megalopolis. Demographic skills can enable us to understand the problem of overpopulation, and without such understanding the problem is unlikely to be resolved. Medical research and biochemical techniques are vital for a satisfactory resolution of the urgent contraceptive problem. All these involve secular skills and sciences. But these cannot of themselves solve the problem of overpopulation. There are tremendous cultural, spiritual, and religious factors involved. Delight in fertility is deeply implanted in normal men and women, witness the pleasure that a new birth gives: it is customary to offer congratulations almost without thinking. Up to the present the principal religions of the world, including most of the principal churches of Christendom, have contributed little if nothing on the religious level to the solution of this great problem; and yet they *must* play their part, for without their aid the problem will not be solved, and the danger to mankind will still remain.

Thirdly I suggested that there must be knowledge of the coming crisis that hangs over man's future. This is partly a secular matter, for the knowledge about man's environment is secular knowledge, gained through secular research and communicated through the ordinary secular channels of communication. I said in the second lecture that no one can be expected to exercise self-control on behalf of posterity without being convinced that such self-control is essential for the sake of posterity. I asked whether such self-control was possible; and the answer surely must lie in the religious sphere. Only if the will and the imagination and the feelings are fully harnessed is mankind likely to change its ways for the sake of unborn generations. How else can such self-control be effected except by the mustering of all the moral and spiritual resources of mankind? We must have a renewal of belief that all men are accountable before God for their stewardship over the created world.

I suggested also that our material standard of living might have to drop, at least in the developed countries of the world. Is this possible? In part this is a secular question. At the moment all economies seem to be geared to greater and greater production. This holds not merely for capitalist systems but also for socialist economies. How can an economy remain healthy without increasing productivity? I do not know the answer to such a technical question. I do not know if there is an answer to such a question; but it seems clear that unless an answer is found, the question mark hanging over man cannot be removed. But a reduction in living standards would be much more than a secular problem. Unless people are content with a lower standard of material living (or at any rate content not to increase their present standard of living) no change will take place. How can they be content? Only if they see this world as not only valuable in itself, but a stepping-stone to man's ultimate goal in eternity. In this perspective, I have suggested, bigger and better material possessions do not seem to be so important. 'A man's life consisteth not in the abundance of the things which he possesseth' (Luke 12:15). Let the churches here take heed; for they cannot effectively show the hollowness of materialism unless they practise what they preach.

Fifthly, I suggested that steps must be taken to see that the natural and instinctive drives of men can have healthy and creative outlets. In part this is a matter of secular skill and knowledge. For example, traumatic experiences in infancy are likely to reduce the growth of a healthy and mature personality; and for avoiding such experiences, skill and knowledge are needed. In the same way modern knowledge can channel into healthy and creative outlets many of man's instinctive drives which otherwise may imperil his future. Here only a few examples must suffice. Competitive sport may supply the kind of ritualised conflict that satisfies man's aggressive drives. Grooming instincts can find satisfaction in other directions than increasing material comfort. Feeding instincts can be modified by dietary knowledge and cultural fashions. Rearing instincts can be modified through changing conventions and fresh light from psychological and sociological studies. All these things can help. But once again more than knowledge and nurture is needed. I suggested that man's integrative drives can only be fully satisfied by faith in a loving and purposeful Creator who vitalises and energises the cosmos and who cares for and loves the individual people who have emerged within the evolutionary process within which his Spirit is at work. What of our other instinctive drives?

Do we not need a hero figure with whom we can identify and to whom we can attempt to approximate? A Christian naturally believes that God has given mankind just such a person in the living, crucified and risen Jesus: indeed he believes that in him God disclosed himself as far as is possible in human personality. Here the Christian not only finds liberation from bondage to his past, but also inspiration for his future. The words and deeds of Christ were no doubt conditioned by the human culture of the age in which he lived, and it would be idle to pretend that everything that he said and did is relevant in itself to our present condition. Yet, for all the historical inadequacies of the Gospels, they depict a Man who bursts through their pages, and who impresses himself upon the reader as one whose inward energies all found a healthy and creative outlet. He is the Proper Man, and by identifying with him at the deepest level of their being men of all ages can find help (or grace) towards their own maturity As for those who find it impossible for cultural or psychological reasons, to make this identification, the eternal Word of God is not without witness in human personality apart from the Incarnate Lord himself.

Such a statement about the past needs qualifying, as most theological statements need qualification. 'Jesus Christ is the same, yesterday, today and for ever.' But we cannot here attempt a rounded picture of belief, only a sketch such as is relevant to our theme. Yet even to point back to the historical Jesus in the past raises questions about man in the future, questions which can here only be barely raised. Biochemical knowledge and medical techniques raise questions about how far it is legitimate for man to alter not just his environment, but himself. Such questions were lightly touched on in a symposium called *Biology and Personality*.[26] A recent issue of the periodical *Contact* (No. 22, February 1968) raised an interesting series of 'Ethical Issues of the 1970's', including such subjects as the control of reproduction, and doctors' dilemmas. These themes have been spelled out with greater precision by G. Rattray Taylor in his book *The Biological Time Bomb*.[27] His chapter headings tell their tale: 'Where are Biologists Taking Us?', 'Is Sex Necessary?', 'The Modified Man', 'Is Death Necessary?', 'New Minds for Old', 'The Genetic Engineers', 'Can We Create Life?'[28] Like all problems concerning human personality, these subjects raise moral and spiritual problems, and it is the moral and spiritual factor that must predominate in decisions about biological engineering. Perhaps a useful question may be: how does a modified man of the future compare with the past figure of Jesus of Nazareth? Man must take care that in altering and modifying a human person, he does not dehumanise him. Mankind always needs a norm, and the humanity of Jesus may be a helpful touchstone as we try to formulate and solve some of these difficult medical dilemmas. To say this may not be to say much; but at least it is to say something in a situation where at present there is little creative thinking.

At this point I should try to recall what has been attempted in these lectures. First a brief statement was made of the dangers from his environment which man is causing. Secondly an attempt was made to analyse the reasons for these dangers from within, that is to say, to consider the drives which lead men to a situation where such dangers become possible. Finally, an attempt has been made to see whether or not the Christian revelation has any useful contribution to make to this crucial question.

What if there is in fact no possibility of averting these dangers? What would then be a Christian attitude towards the future? If *Homo sapiens* were to commit specific suicide, this would really make no difference to the problem that evil poses to the theist, except perhaps in quantitive terms. It seems that in any case the species will perish later if not sooner. We cannot say that this would defeat the purposes of God for the world, because we do not know what his purposes are: we cannot see the point of history until history has ended. When the authors of the 1662 English Prayer Book composed their work, they certainly thought that the world would go on and on almost for ever; but then it is well known that the Church of England seems to be 'as it was in the beginning, is now and ever shall be, world without end'! At any rate, if you have ever whiled away time during a tedious sermon by looking at the tables to determine the date of Easter at the beginning of the Prayer Book, you will see that the list does not merely end at the Year of our Lord 8500, but (as in the original manuscript) the list ends with the year 8500 *etc.* They thought that man would last that long. In the most recent proposals for the Church's year, the last date given for Easter is A.D. 2000![29] But not so in the primitive Church; in the primitive Church and indeed in the time of Jesus expectation was very short. The world was expected to end soon, and this was seen as part of God's providence, and indeed part of his mercy and judgement. The same will be true if man cannot shortly avoid the perils that he is bringing on himself.

But there is no necessity to be pessimistic. If the outlook is not good, it is certainly not hopeless. I have tried to suggest that, with a great effort, a spiritual and moral effort as well as a scientific and technological effort, our dangers could be overcome. We have not surely yet reached the point of no return, although it may be that it is not very far off. We must be grateful to UNESCO for bringing the matter to the attention of its representatives. We must be grateful that so far countries who in other ways have opposed each other's interests are in this matter beginning to show co-operation and concern. We must be glad too that the United Nations have decided to hold special sessions on this crucial matter in 1972. And yet we must not expect too much from these bodies. The policies of UNESCO and UNO are decided by the member states who comprise them, and their officials can, by the nature of the case, be little more than the equivalent of civil servants. If mankind is to be aroused to take action in the face of these growing dangers, a huge moral and spiritual impetus is needed that can never be found in political and social organisations.

Where is the initiative to be found? Is it too much to hope that there could be a real attempt made by a leader of a Christian church to gather together men of all religions and indeed men of good will to initiate this moral and spiritual impetus that is so badly needed? Surely this would be time better spent by the Churches than their apparently endless conferences and commissions on matters doctrinal or ecclesiastical. Here the Church could truly serve the world. Is this using religion because of the world's needs? Does it really matter if it is? I have urged that unless man comes to the conviction of his accountability before God, and his stewardship over nature, his future remains in doubt; and unless man sees this world in the perspective of eternity, his material values will be false. Does it really matter that it takes a crisis of unparalleled dimensions for man to come to the knowledge of the truth?

Who could summon such a conference? It might be preferable for the call to come from a new Ecumenical Council, or from the General Assembly of the World Council of Churches; but this hardly seems practicable. On the other hand, Resolution 6 of the 1968 Lambeth Conference runs as follows:

The Conference urges all Christians, in obedience to the doctrine of creation, to take all possible action to ensure man's responsible stewardship over nature; in particular in his relationship with animals, and with regard to the conservation of soil, and the prevention of the pollution of air, soil and ocean.

And according to Resolution 11, 'the Christian Churches must endeavour such positive relationship to the different religions of man, as will ... encourage Christians to increasing co-operation with men of other faiths in the fields of economic, social and moral action'.

Is it too much to hope that our Archbishop of Canterbury, in the spirit of these resolutions, should begin consultations

with the spiritual and moral leaders of mankind, for a conference complementary to that of the United Nations?

Nothing less than the future of the whole of mankind is
at stake.

*Lecture delivered 29 January 1969, under the title 'Towards a
Theology of the Future'.*

NOTES

Lecture 1

1. Limited prognosis has been attempted elsewhere. Cf. the first materials to come from the Commission on the Year 2000 set up by the American Academy of Arts and Sciences and published in *Daedalus* 96 (No. 3), 1967; also the Annual Reports of Resources for the Future, Inc.

1ᴬ. *The Times*, 27 December 1968.

2. *The Times*, 20 February 1968.

3. Lord Ritchie-Calder, *Hell Upon Earth*, 23 November 1968, p. 7.

4. Cf. *The Times*, 28 March 1968; C. G. Hedén, 'The Infectious Dust-cloud', in *Unless Peace Comes*, ed. N. Calder (Allen Lane, London, 1968), p. 140.

5. *Conservation and Rational Use of the Environment*, a report prepared for FAO and UNESCO (1967), p. 25.

6. Intergovernmental Conference of Experts on the Scientific Basis for Rational Use and Conservation of the Resources of the Biosphere, referred to hereafter as the Biosphere Conference.

7. Op. cit., IV, 18 (a), p. 5.

8. Speech to the General Assembly of the United Nations, 3 December 1968.

9. *Water Resources Problems* (Biosphere Conference), p. 3.

10. Ibid., p. 15.

11. Ibid., p. 5.

12. Lord Ritchie-Calder, op. cit., p. 14.

13. *Conservation and Rational Use of the Environment*, p. 71.

14. *The Times*, 5 March 1968. Erosion continues elsewhere. Lord Byers

said recently in the House of Lords: 'The Sahara desert in West Africa is advancing at the rate of nearly twenty miles a year' (*Hansard*, 19 February 1969, col. 822).

15. G. Schwab, *Dance with the Devil* (Bles, London, 1963), p. 123.

16. Ibid., p. 125.

17. Ibid., p. 111.

18. Professor G. W. Dimbleby, 'Man's Impact on his Environment', lecture to the British Association, 1965.

19. Schwab, op. cit., p. 121.

20. Ibid., p. 117.

21. *Conservation and Rational Use of the Environment*, p. 11.

22. R. S. R. Fitter, *Vanishing Wild Animals of the World* (Kaye & Ward, London, 1968), p. 20.

23. K. Mellanby, *Pesticides and Pollution* (Collins, London, 1967), pp. 17f.

24. Fitter, op. cit., p. 17.

25. According to the Red Book Data of the Survival Service Commission of the International Union for Conservation of Nature.

26. Private communication from the International Union for Conservation of Nature.

27. *Protection of Rare and Endangered Species* (Biosphere Conference), p. 11.

28. Biosphere Conference, *Final Report*, V, 50, p. 11.

29. *Protection of Rare and Endangered Species* (Biosphere Conference), p. 11.

30. According to figures published in 1968 by the *Statistic Review of World Oil Industry* (BP).

31. *The Times*, Business section, 8 February 1968.

32. Sir Stanley Brown, Chairman of the Central Electricity Generating Board, 1 January 1968.

33. According to the published survey of the Chase Manhattan Bank (1968).

34. *Sunday Times*, 23 February 1969.

35. *The Times*, 17 February 1969.

36. *CEGB Newsletter* No. 77, May 1968.

37. *CEGB Newsletter* No. 63, February 1966.

38. Biosphere Conference, *Final Report*, III, 16, p. 4.

39. Mellanby, op. cit., p. 16.

40. Lord Caradon, speech to the General Assembly of the United Nations, 3 December 1968.

41. *Problems of Deterioration of the Environment* (Biosphere Conference), p. 18.

42. Mellanby, op. cit., p. 25.

43. Ibid., p. 71.

44. *Daily Mail*, 30 December 1968.

45. *Sunday Times*, 29 December 1968.

46. Op. cit., p. 9.

47. *Problems of the Deterioration of the Environment* (Biosphere Conference), p. 4.

48. *The Disposal of Fission Product Wastes by Incorporation Into Glass* (AERE, 1960).

49. *Radioactive Waste Disposal into the Atlantic 1967* (OECD, 1968).

50. Op. cit., p. 10.

51. *Euratom*, Vol. VI, no. 1, March 1967, p. 25.

52. *Euratom*, Vol. VI, no. 3, September 1967, p. 84.

53. *Euratom*, ibid.

54. *Problems of the Deterioration of the Environment* (Biosphere Conference), p. 5.

55. Mr Aström, Swedish Representative at the UN, speech to the General Assembly, 3 December 1968.

56. Mr Kaplan, Canadian Representative at the UN, speech to the General Assembly, 3 December 1968.

57. *Guardian*, 11 February 1969.

58. Mr Wiggins, US Representative to the UN, speech to the General Assembly, 3 December 1968.

59. Schwab, op. cit., p. 62.

60. Hamilton, London, 1963.

61. Biosphere Conference, *Final Report*, VI, 60, p. 13.

62. *Problems of the Deterioration of the Environment* (Biosphere Conference), p. 17.

63. Mr Aström, UN General Assembly, 3 December 1968.

64. *Guardian*, 29 December 1968. The average American has 12 p.p.m. DDT in his fatty tissues, but meat with only 7 p.p.m. is thought unfit to eat! (*Guardian*, 24 April 1969). Mother's milk actually contains twice as much DDT as is permitted in commercial milk (*Guardian*, 25 June 1969).

65. *Observer*, 2 March 1969.

66. *Guardian*, 29 December 1968.

67. Mr Aström, UN General Assembly, 3 December 1968.

68. *Conservation and Rational Use of the Environment*, p. 26.

69. Mr Aström, UN General Assembly, 3 December 1968.

70. *Problems of the Deterioration of the Environment* (Biosphere Conference), p. 12.

71. Mr Aström, UN General Assembly, 3 December 1968.

72. *Problems of the Deterioration of the Environment* (Biosphere Conference), p. 9.

73. Ibid., p. 11.

74. Ibid., p. 10.

75. Ibid., p. 11.

76. Ibid., p. 10.

77. Ibid., pp. 9f.

78. Ibid.

79. Ibid., p. 10.

80. Mr Wiggins, UN General Assembly, 3 December 1968.

81. Mr Aström, UN General Assembly, 3 December 1968.

82. Ibid.

83. *Conservation and Rational Use of the Environment*, p. 26.

84. Lord Ritchie-Calder, op. cit., p. 12.

85. Mr. Aström, UN General Assembly, 3 December 1968.

86. Op. cit., p. 12.

87. *The Times*, 20 February 1968.

88. Op cit., p. 12.

88A. Since this lecture was delivered, attention has been drawn to a further possible source of contamination through the introduction by returning astronauts of resistant micro-organisms. Professor Alexander has commented, 'Complete sterility is often impossible to achieve.' (*Nature*, 3 May 1969, p. 432).

89. Dr Candau, Director-General of WHO, 4 September 1968.

90. *Guardian*, 19 October 1968.

91. R. Dubos, 'Environment and Health' in *Environmental Quality in a Growing Economy* (John Hopkins Press, Baltimore, 1966), p. 31.

92. Mr Boerma, Director-General of FAO, 4 September 1968. A recent report has suggested that one person in five in this country suffers from obesity. In the USA the proportion is as high as one in three! Cf. N. W. Pirie, *Food Resources Conventional and Novel* (Pelican, London, 1969), p. 83.

93. Ibid.

94. One ton of leaves can produce 40 lb of protein concentrate, supplying one tenth of the daily protein needs of 50,000 people (cf. *The Times*, 19 July 1968). Problems of gathering and distribution would be insuperable on a huge scale.

95. Mr Boerma, 4 September 1968.

96. Ibid.

97. Cf. W. and P. Paddock, *Famine 1975!* (Weidenfeld & Nicolson, London, 1968).

98. Cf. H. Nicol, *The Limits of Man* (Constable, London, 1967).

99. *Qualitative and Quantitative Living Space Requirements* (Biosphere Conference), *Final Report*, Annex IV, p. 2.

100. Ibid., p. 3.

101. R. Dubos, op. cit., p. 27.

102. Dr W. Sargant, presidential address to a World Psychiatric Association symposium, 13 November 1967.

103. *The Times*, 14 November 1967.

104. *Nature*, 219 (1968), p. 765.

105. By Mr R. I. F. Brown of Glasgow University's psychosomatic research unit (cf. *The Times*, 28 March 1968).

106. R. Dubos, op. cit., p. 38.

107. Ibid., p. 39.

108. S. A. Barnett, 'Physiological Effects of "Social Stress" in Wild Rats – I', *Journal of Psychosomatic Research*, 1958, Vol. 3, pp. 1–11.

109. Cf. P. A. Cresswell and G. A. Smith, *Student Suicide* (1968).

110. According to the 1967 report of the GLC scientific adviser, the Thames and the air in London are getting cleaner.

111. *The Registrar-General's Decennial Supplement, England and Wales*, 1961, Life Tables, p. 13.

112. H. Selye, *The Stress of Life* (McGraw-Hill, New York, 1956), p. 3.

113. Ibid., pp. 48–127.

114. Ibid., pp. 128–214.

115. Dr Candau, 4 September 1968.

116. E. Huxley, *Brave New Victuals* (Chatto & Windus, London, 1965), pp. 49ff.

117. Selye, op. cit.

118. *Animal Dispersion in Relation to Social Behaviour* (Oliver & Boyd, Edinburgh, 1962).

119. Cf. D. Chitty, 'Self-regulation of Numbers through Changes in Viability', *Cold Spring Harbour Symp.* quant. Biol. 22 (1957), 277–80; S. A. Barnett *et al.*, 'Physiological Effects of "Social Stress" in Wild Rats – II', *Journal of Psychosomatic Research*, 1960, pp. 251–60.

120. 'The Sane Community – a Density Problem?', *Discovery*, September 1965.

121. P. Leyhausen, 'Communal Organization of Solitary Mammals', *Symp. Zool. Soc. 14* (1965), pp. 244–63.

122. F. H. McClintock and N. H. Avison, *Crime in England and Wales* (Heinemann, London, 1968), Table 2.2, p. 23.

123. Ibid., p. 24. They also point out that the two are not necessarily interconnected.

124. Cf. N. Timms, *Rootless in the City* (National Council for Social Service, London, January 1969).

125. *Violence, Monkeys and Man* (Macmillan, London, 1968).

126. P. Leyhausen, 'The Sane Community'.

127. R. Dubos, op. cit., p. 29.

128. Ibid., p. 23.

129. Biosphere Conference, *Final Report*, V, 50, p. 11.

Lecture 2

1. *The Ghost in the Machine* (Hutchinson, London, 1967), p. 322.

2. *Qualitative and Quantitative Living Space Requirements*, Biosphere Conference, *Final Report*, Annex IV, p. 4.

3. A good introduction to many aspects of the coming crisis may be found in Robert Arvill, *Man and Environment* (Pelican, London, 1967).

4. *Science and Survival* (Gollancz, London, 1966), p. 100.

5. Op cit., p. 288.

6. It is good to know that the Church of England's Board for Social Responsibility has now set up a working-party on the Relationship between the Different Orders of Creation, which is due to report early in 1970.

7. Biosphere Conference, *Final Report*, II, 12, p. 4.

8. Op. cit., IV, 18 (c), p. 5.

9. *Qualitative and Quantitative Living Space Requirements*, Biosphere Conference, *Final Report*, Annex IV, p. 1.

10. Op. cit., p. 11.

11. *A Runaway World?*, (BBC, London, 1968), p. 1.

12. Ibid., p. 6.

13. Ibid., p. 9.

14. Isa. 55:6–7. (R.V.)

15. Jer. 3:14. (R.V.)

16. Amos 5:4. (R.V.)

17. Gen. 1:26–7. (R.V.)

18. Ps. 8:5 f. (R.V.)

19. Cf. my 'Man's Dominion' in *The Responsible Church*, ed. E. Barker (SPCK, London, 1966), p. 78.

20. Gen. 2:7.

21. Cf. Rom. 8:18 ff. For an exposition of this passage, cf. C. F. D. Moule, *Man and Nature in the New Testament* (Athlone, London, 1964).

22. Gen. 1:28. (R.V.)

23. Cf. Sir Alister Hardy, *The Living Stream* (Collins, London, 1965).

24. Cf. K. Lorenz, *On Aggression* (Methuen, London, 1966); D. Morris, *The Naked Ape* (Cape, London, 1967).

25. W. H. Thorpe, 'Ethology and Consciousness' in *Brain and Conscious Experience*, ed. J. C. Eccles (New York, 1966), pp. 470–505.

26. K. Lorenz, op. cit., p. 208.

27. R. Ardrey, *African Genesis* (Collins, London, 1961).

28. A. Storr, *Human Aggression* (Allen Lane, London, 1968), p. 114.

29. Cf. *Man and Aggression*, ed. M. F. Ashley Montague (OUP, London, 1968).

30. Cf. R. A. Hinde, 'The Nature of Aggression', *New Society*, 2 March 1967, pp. 302ff.; 'Aggression Again,' ibid., 20 February 1969, pp. 291f.

31. D. W. Winnicott, *Collected Papers* (Tavistock, London, 1958), .204.

32. A. Storr, op. cit., Introduction.

33. S. A. Barnett, 'Aggression and Defence', *UCLA Forum in Medical ciences*, No. 7 (Berkeley, 1967).

34. A. Koestler, op. cit., p. 233.

35. Ibid., p. 234.

36. Ibid., p. 245.

37. Ibid., p. 259.

38. Ibid., pp. 265–6.

39. W. E. Le Gros Clark, 'The Humanity of Man', in *The Advancement of Science* XVII, No. 73 (1961), p. 217.

40. Cf. A. T. W. Simeons, *Man's Presumptuous Brain* (Longmans, London, 1960).

41. Bernard Towers, however, calls this account 'so replete with anatomical misconceptions as to make the conclusions worthless' (*Concerning Teilhard*, Collins, London, 1969, p. 226).

Lecture 3

1. D. M. MacKinnon *et al.* (Constable, London, 1963), pp. 82f.

2. Cf. my 'Jesus the Revelation of God' in *Christ For Us Today*, ed, N. Pittenger (SCM, London, 1968), pp. 107ff.

3. Cf. J. Baillie, *And the Life Everlasting* (OUP, London, 1934), pp. 268ff.

4. J. A. T. Robinson, *In the End God* (Fontana, London, 1968), p. 135.

5. J. Moltmann, *Theology of Hope* (SCM, London, 1968), p. 17.

6. *The Nature and Destiny of Man*, Vol. II (Nisbet, London, 1943), pp. 300f.

7. *Eternal Hope* (Lutterworth, London, 1954), pp. 108ff.

8. *The Christian Hope* (Longmans, London, 1954), p. 221.

9. (Lutterworth, London, 1968), p. 137.

10. (Lutterworth, London 1968), pp. 166, 177.

11. *The Secular City* (SCM, London, 1965), p. 110.

12. Ibid., p. 113.

13. A. M. Ramsey, *God, Christ and the World* (SCM, London, 1969), p. 25.

14. *The Future of Man* (Methuen, London, 1960), p. 53.

15. Cf. Masatoshi Nei, *Nature* 221 (1969), p. 40.

16. *The Nature of the Universe* (Blackwell, Oxford, 1950), p. 86.

17. Ibid., p. 37.

18. Teilhard de Chardin, *The Future of Man* (Collins, London, 1964), p. 299.

19. Ibid., p. 300.

20. Ibid., p. 302.

21. Ibid., pp. 236f.

22. Dr Bernard Towers, replying to Dr Medawar's attack on Teilhard in the January 1961 issue of *Mind*, speaks of him as a scientific pioneer rather than as a master of science (*The Listener*, 15 April 1965, p. 557; reprinted in Bernard Towers, *Concerning Teilhard* (Collins, London, 1969), p. 89).

23. Op cit., p. 231n.

24. Ibid., pp. 122f.

25. Epistle I, IX, 267–80.

26. Ed. I. T. Ramsey (Blackwell, Oxford, 1965).

27. Thames and Hudson, London, 1968.

28. More recently Mr Herman Kahn of the Hudson Institute, speaking in London, predicted systems of direct communication with the brain which

would enable the pleasure centres to be stimulated electronically (*The Times*, 16 May 1969).

29. *The Calendar and Lessons for the Church's Year. A Report of the Church of England Liturgical Commission* (SPCK, London, 1969), p. 29. The Commission expects that sometime there will be a fixed date for Easter.

ACKNOWLEDGEMENTS

The author and publisher wish to acknowledge their indebtedness for permission to reproduce copyright material as follows:-

from 'Intellectual Objections' by J. S. Bezzant in *Objections to Christian Belief*, edited by Rev A. R. Vidler, published by Constable, London, 1963;

from *Science and Survival* by Barry Commoner, published by Victor Gollancz, London, 1966, reprinted by permission of Laurence Pollinger Ltd;

from *Conservation and Rational Use of the Environment,* a report prepared for FAO and UNESCO, 1967;

from 'Environment and Health' by R. Dubos in *Environmental Quality in a Growing Economy*, published by the John Hopkins Press, Baltimore, 1966;

from *The Ghost in the Machine* by Arthur Koestler, published by Hutchinson, London, 1967, reprinted by permission of A. D. Peters & Company;

from *A Runaway World?* by Dr. E. R. Leach, published by BBC Publications, London, 1968;

from the Report on *Problems of Deterioration of the Environment,* the Report on *Water Resources Problems* and the *Final Report* of the Intergovernmental Conference of Experts on the Scientific Basis for Rational Use and Conservation of the Resources of the Biosphere, UNESCO, Paris, 1968.

It should be noted that the extracts from speeches made at the 23rd Session of the General Assembly of the United Nations are taken from the provisional verbatim records which may be subject to amendment before final publication.

INDEX

99